BUSINESS COMMUNICATION

BUSINESS COMMUNICATION

Dr. Debasish Biswas
M.Com, MBA, M.Phil, DLL, PGDHM,
GDCA,PGDE, PGDMM, PGDFM, Ph.D.
Assistant Professor& Head
Department of Business Administration
Vidyasagar University, Midnapore, W.B.
&
Dr.Dipa Banerjee
MBA, Ph.D.

Business Communication

Edition:2026

ISBN 978-93-87537-86-6

Published by:
CRESCENT PUBLISHING CORPORATION
4806/24, Mathur Lane,
Ansari Road, Darya Ganj,
New Delhi - 110 002
Ph.: 011 - 23244131
Mob.: + 91 - 9711991838, 9999021668
E-mail: crescentbook@gmail.com
Website: www.crescentpublishingcorp.weebly.com

Printed at:
Roshan Offset Printers
Delhi

PRINTED IN INDIA

Dedicated to our beloved students

Preface

It is indeed a real fact that in the past, the blow of a sward was a threat to all. But the scenario has changed drastically and today communication for both 'verbal' and 'nonverbal' seems to be mightier than a sword.

The concept of 'communication' is as old as human civilization. From the ancient age, man has realized the necessity to transmit the information, ideas and concept. Afterwards, the theory and practices of communication was a main concern of Greek, Roman, Medieval, Renaissance and early modern education. Man has been using language as a tool of communication. Today, language is a valued asset of man.

Our sincere and deliberate efforts have been devoted to give the book a comprehensive form. All chapters have been discussed in a very simple and lucid language so as to make the subject easily understandable to our readers.

We feel great pleasure in placing the first edition of this book before our esteemed readers. It is the outcome of a great deal of encouragement from our colleagues and request from students.

This book is appropriate for commerce and management students at graduate and post graduate level of different Indian Universities.

We welcome suggestions from esteemed teachers and students for enrichment and improvement of the book in the future.

Debasish Biswas
Dipa Banerjee

Acknowledgements

First of all, we would like to express our sincere gratitude to Prof. (Dr.) Debabrata Mitra, Department of Commerce, University of North Bengal, who has been our motivator since the beginning of our write up. He provided us with many helpful suggestions, important advice and constant encouragement during the course of this work.

A special note of appreciation is due to Prof. (Dr.) Susanta Mitra, professor of Commerce, Kazi Nazrul University, West Bengal for his valuable contributions towards enhancing the standard of the book.

We are grateful to the esteemed teachers who always provided us with their valuable suggestions from time to time. We are thankful to our students who always shown a keen interest in our publication. We offer our heartfelt congratulations to **Crescent Publishing Corporation** for their untiring effort and support in bringing out this book.

We also thank to Dr. Nirmal Chandra Roy, The University of Burdwan, West Bengal for extending help in conducting the task.

The responsibility for errors remains us alone.

Debasish Biswas
Dipa Banerjee

Contents

Chapter-1

Fundamentals of Communication

Contents

1.0: Learning Objectives

After studying this unit, you will be able to

- Understand the meaning, definitions, and purpose of communication;

- Comprehend the features and importance of communication;
- Know various types of communication;
- Appreciate the channels of communication;
- Understand various barriers to effective communication.

1.1: Concept and Meaning of Communication

"A blow with a word strikes deeper than a blow with a sward"

-Robert Burton

It is indeed a real fact that in the past, the blow of a sward was a threat to all. However, the scenario has been changed drastically and nowadays; both 'verbal' and 'nonverbal' communication seems to be mightier than a sword.

The conception of 'communication' is as old as human civilization. From the ancient age, human community has realized the necessity to transmit the information, ideas, and concept. Afterwards, the theory and practices of communication were a main concern of Greek, Roman, Medieval, Renaissance, and early modern education. Man has been using several languages as one of the important tools of communication. Today, language has become a valuable asset in the hands of human community.

'Communication' acts as a 'storehouse of knowledge', a 'propeller for the progression of knowledge' and a 'telescope to visualize the future'. Presently, our society moves on the 'wheels of communication'. In this professional world, communication skill of an individual plays a very significant role to reach the apex level of the career graph in one's life.

One's better communication skill will bring success to his/her goals in life. 'Communication' may be of two types. One is verbal and the other one is nonverbal communication. In the case of verbal communication, listeners or receivers can understand what speakers or senders are saying. On the contrary, the written communication is expected to be clear, focused, and brief with corrected words.

A business firm can get its relevant information from the 'written communication'. It also provides a chance to employees to put their suggestions through writing. Naturally, effective communication is very important for success of an organization. Every business organization has certain specified objectives. To accomplish these objectives, the co-ordination among the employees of an organization is essential. It is only possible through effective communication.

Communication is one of the major functions of management for any organization. This is a process of sending out information, ideas, thoughts, opinions, and plans among various departments of any business organization. Effective communication is required for maintaining good human relations within the organization and successfully run a business organization. Effective communication is also required to maintain the employer-employee relations.

1.2: Definition

The word 'communication' has a rich history. The word 'communication' originates from Latin word 'communicare' which means to share. Various authors and researchers define the term 'communication' in their own way. Some of them are quoted as under:

According to Koontz and O'Donnell, "Communication is an intercourse by words, letters, symbols or messages; and is a way that one organization member shares meaning and understanding with another."

Brown has defined communication as "A process of transmitting ideas or thoughts from one person to another for the purpose of creating understanding in the thinking of the person receiving the message."

Allen Louis A. defines Communication as "It is a sum of all the things one person does when he wants to create understanding in the minds of another. It involves a systematic and continuous process of telling, listening and understanding."

In the words of **Theo Haimann**, "Communication is the process of passing information and understanding from one person to another. It is the process of imparting ideas and making oneself understood by others."

From the above definitions, we can precisely say that it is a methodical and continuous process of exchange of facts and ideas, which help an individual or organization to share their views with each other.

Therefore, it can be concluded that communication is not simply the transmission of message but also plays a vital role for correct interpretation and understanding.

1.3: Purpose of Professional Communication

The communication has its manifold aspects which have been described below:

1. Providing Instruction: Instruction is a particular type of order which is generally given to the subordinates by the higher authorities and it also guides the subordinates so that they can execute the order in an efficient and effective way. The authority gives orders or instructions to their subordinates with the help of effective mode of communication.

2. Integration: The integration function of communication mainly involves in carrying out inter-relationship among the various departmental functions of the business organization. It helps in amalgamation of various functions of management.

3. Evaluation Process: It is a tool to appraise an individual or the team about their contribution to the organization.

4. Giving Orders: Giving order is an authoritative communication. Communication is required to issue orders by the senior level employees to the lower level employees. The directions may be given either verbally or in writing. Ordering however is an art that requires effective communication skill.

5. Influencing Others: An effective communication process is required in influencing others or being influenced. The individual having excellent communication skill can easily influence others.

6. Projecting Image: A business enterprise cannot separate its business from the society. There is an interrelationship between the society and enterprise. The goodwill of a business is mainly dependent on the brand image which can be created through effective communication.

7. Employees Orientation: When an incumbent joins to an organization, he or she requires proper orientation so that he or she can understand about the organizational values, norms, policies, culture, objectives, etc.

8. Staffing: Communication is required for recruitment and selection process. The recruiters provide information about the company's vision, mission, objective, policies, practices, etc. to the applicants. In this way, it helps the new entrants to get an idea about the organization.

9. Raising Morale: Morale is the mental health of individuals which is necessary for the development of an organization. It acts as a kind of lubricant among people, knit them with a sense of togetherness and force them to work in the best interest of their organization. Morale is to be preserved only through effective communication.

1.4: Features of Successful Professional Communication

It is obvious that the managers of an organization spends about 80 per cent of his time in communication such as reading various reports, giving verbal or written instruction to the subordinates, conducting meeting, listening to the grievances, etc. Alvin Dodd has rightly remarked that "the number one management problem today is communication."

Since communication has its impact on the professional world, it's essential to get acquainted with the most important features of successful professional communication.

1. Communication is basically a two way process by which information is communicated to the individual and / or organization.

2. It has been seen that the role of the receiver and the sender keeps on changing in the whole process of communication.

3. Communication comprises of verbal and nonverbal forms. Therefore, it includes lip reading, figure –spelling, sign language and body language used in face to face communication.

4. It is a process which transmits the important ideas, thoughts, plans, feelings, etc.

5. Communication skills are considered as an art of techniques of persuasion with the help of verbal and nonverbal features.

A model of communication process can be explained in the following figure.

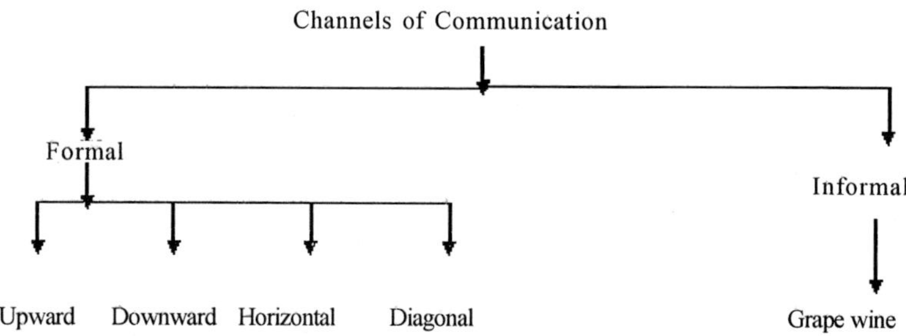

Fig. 1.1: Model of a Communication Process

1.5: Importance

Communication is essential in today's business world. It is said that the world of modern management is the world of communication. The importance of communication can be explained in the following ways:

1. Helps in Smooth Running of a Business: This is "an age of specialization" where in a business different activities are been carried out by different departments like production, stores, marketing and sales, advertising, financing, HR etc. Naturally a proper coordination is necessary for smooth running of a business.

For instance, when production is fully geared up, stores may report shortage of raw materials.

Similarly, the Finance Department has to appraise the other departments regarding its constraints so that the other department can plan accordingly for the future course of action. In fact, all the departments need to keep communication with each other to achieve organizational goals.

2. Communication is a Tool of Sharing Information: The main purpose of communication is to inform the individual or group about the specific job or company policies, procedures, etc. Information can flow horizontally, vertically, and diagonally across the organization. Top management informs policies to the middle management and subsequently it reaches to the lower level. On the other hand, the lower level informs the reaction to the top level through the middle level. Thus, communication acts as a tool of sharing information in an organization.

3. Develop Cooperation and Mutual Understanding: The cooperation among the employees develop through communication. The good communication between the employees and the management brings about an atmosphere of mutual trust and faith. Through effective communication, employees get job satisfaction and a sense of belongingness with the organization which ultimately leads to the success of an organization.

4. Facilitate Employees for Better Performance: It is needed to enable the employees to perform their functions effectively. Employees are required to know their job. This knowledge makes it easy for them to identify themselves with the organizational objectives.

5. Helps Manager to Perform: Communication helps the managers to perform his managerial functions which include planning, organizing, staffing, directing, and controlling. The manager uses communication as a specific tool for sharing information. By using this tool, he organizes the people, gives his directives to the subordinates, motivates, and guides them to complete the job.

6. Communication is a Tool of Coordination: Communication is an effective tool for coordination among workers in order to achieve the organizational goals.

7. Communication is a Tool for Motivation and Morale: It is also a basic tool for motivation which can improve morale of the employees. On the other hand, wrong or faulty communication among employees or between manager and his subordinates is the main cause of conflict which ultimately results in low morale at work.

8. Maintaining Good Human Relations: With effective communication, the organization can uphold good human relations among the employees. Managers encourage their employees so that employees can give their best ideas and suggestions. The best ideas or suggestions are implemented to enhance the production and to minimize the cost.

9. Helps to Maintain Industrial Peace and Harmony: Sometimes, it is observed that improper communication may result in industrial disputes between management and workers. Through effective communication, management and workers can put their views with each other to maintain the industrial peace and harmony in the organization.

10. Helps in Projecting the Image of the Enterprise: In modern business scenario, it is very important to project the image of the organization in the society. An organization used to get support from the society due to the information flow to the society about the organizational goals and activities.

From the above discussion, it can be concluded that an appropriate approach of communication is necessary for the survival and smooth functioning of an organization.

1.6: Types of Communication

It can be broadly classified into the following types:

Verbal communication, nonverbal communication, intrapersonal communication, interpersonal communication, extra personal communication, mass communication, and media communication

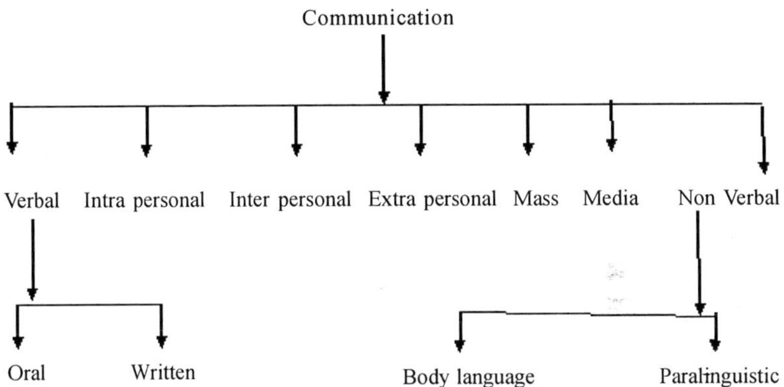

Fig. 1.2: Forms of Communication at a Glance

1. Verbal Communication: A professional person has to deal his /her prime working time in speaking and listening to other person apart from reading and writing. This is a main vehicle of a professional person to transmit his /her message. It is mainly termed as 'verbal communication'. Verbal communication can be divided into two forms –oral and written.

a) Oral Communication: In oral communication, the sender and the receiver interact face to face. Generally two persons or more use this communication as a medium of communication. This mode of communication is used at the time of presentation, deliver speeches, and participate in group discussion.

b) Written Communication: The sender uses this to send the message. Mainly, this communication is used for documentary purpose. The following are included in this category.

- Reports
- Proposals
- Hand books

- Letters
- E-mails

2. Intrapersonal Communication: Whenever communication takes places within an individual, it is called 'Intrapersonal Communication'. Individual reflection, observation, and meditation come under this form of communication.

3. Extra Personal Communication: The communication with non-human entities such as animals, birds, etc. is termed as extra personal communication. For instance, whenever we commend our pet dog or cat to sit, stand or play; they follow the orders.

4. Mass Communication: This is mainly the application of tools of mass media. The example of this communication is books, cinema, press, television, radio, internet, etc.

5. Media Communication: The main tools for media communication are computers, cell phones, LCD, video, television, etc. Presently, internet has become very popular for this communication. It is mainly used in office and personal communication.

6. Nonverbal Communication: In this mode of communication, a message is been communicated without using a word. It plays a vital role in the world of professional communication. It is further divided into two parts: Body Language and Paralinguistic.

a) Body Language includes gesture, posture, facial expression, hand movements, eye contacts, etc.

b) On the other hand, Paralinguistic feature includes a person's voice, modulation, pitch, articulation, etc.

1.7: Channels of Communication

Communication is essential for the effective functioning of any business organization. In order to accomplish the organizational goals, smooth flow of communication is deemed necessary for different people working in an organization.

These channels of communication are classified into informal channel and formal channel.

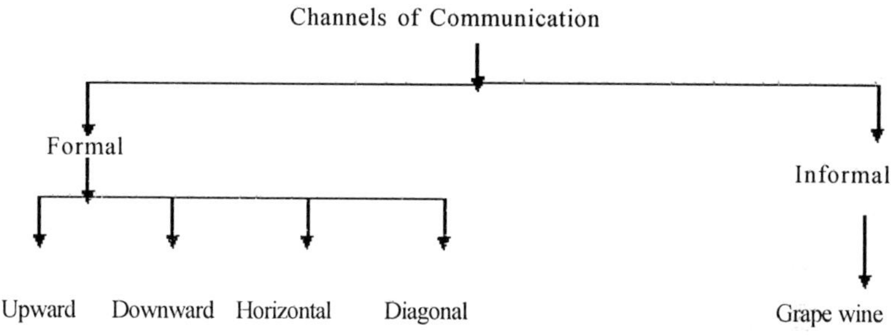

Fig. 1.3: Channels of Communication

Formal Channels of Communication: Formal channels of communication can be segregated into four major channels of communication:

- **Upward**
- **Downward**
- **Horizontal**
- **Diagonal**

Upward Communication: It includes the transmission of information from the subordinates to the seniors. The main use of upward communication is to give proper feedback on various areas of a business unit. A business report sent by the Branch Manager to the Zonal Head of the company is the appropriate instance of upward communication. It offers better working atmosphere within an organization by giving opportunities to the subordinates to share their ideas and views with their bosses. Hence, this channel of communication provides workers' participation in management.

Downward Communication: When a communication comes from higher level to the lower level of employees; it called as downward communication. It is basically deals with direction and control part of a business organization.

A suitable example of 'downward communication' may be given like when a direction or instruction comes from general manager to a purchase manager. It is essential for a business as it involves the instruction, order or advice to the concerned subordinates which will be guidelines for them. Naturally it increases the awareness of the staffs by transmitting the newly implemented company's policy, decision and a positive effect on staff's performance appraisal. Though, this communication channel has to use in a restricted way or else it may hampers the employer-employee relationship.

Horizontal Communication: It occurs between peer group and the people working in the same level of an organization. The main purpose of 'horizontal communication' is to improve team work and thereby promoting the coordination among employees within an organization. It is less formalin nature and more structured than downward communication and upward communication.

Diagonal Communication: It is also termed as "spiral communication". Sometimes, communication flows between persons of various levels of hierarchy and have no direct reporting authority. 'Diagonal communication' flows in all directions. The application of this communication is seen in corporate sector like: IT and Management.

1.8: Barriers to Effective Communication

If we look around carefully, we will find that there are people who do not bother to listen others during personal interaction or in a meeting. Also, it is seen that a few people use to write unstructured notes/memos which is not understandable. It occurs when the communication received is not same as communication sent. Communication barriers arise during the common process and may confuse both the listener and the reader, create misunderstanding and confusion. Let us look upon the different types of communication that affects in smooth running of an enterprise.

Broadly the barriers of communication can be divided into two groups: Verbal barriers and Nonverbal barriers.

- **Verbal Barriers**
- **Non-verbal Barriers**

(A) Verbal Barriers

All most all the people consider themselves a good speaker / communicator. While speaking, one should not feel that speaking fluently is not the essential aspect of communicating rather it is not the prime requirement. Ultimately it leads to verbal barriers like verbal attach, speaking loudly, using complex words. The following reasons may create the verbal barrier in the environment:

1. Lack of Proper Planning While Speaking: Very often we use to see that people start talking or writing without planning. They could not clearly state the purpose of their message. This leads to the miscommunication in the communication process.

2. Language Selection: In our daily professional life, we use to interact with different people and pointless to say that we choose different varieties of expressions. Selection of a wrong variety of language leads to failure as the communicator fails to get the feedback of his/her link and hence the selection of wrong variety of language fails to bring out the desired result.

3. Improper Encoding: Improper encoding is a frequent barrier in communication. Very often, due to improper expression, message does not transmit properly to the receiver. Application of proper words, absence of punctuation marks, insufficient knowledge about the organization, use of jargon, etc. bring ambiguity in the message. It also occurs that the sender has tried to communicate but the receiver may fall into misinterpretation by decoding the message in a different way.

4. Semantic or Language Gap: Sometimes, the gap arises due to much of what people say is subjective or multiple meaning of words or misinterpretation of language. This type of barrier originates in the process of receiving or understanding of the message.

5. Variation in Language: Sometimes, the words and expression are culture specific. If it is not been used properly it might lead barriers in communication process. For example: what is called pavement in Britain; it is called 'sidewalk' in US, whereas in India, it is called 'platform'. Therefore, if we use such expressions haphazardly, it would lead to confusion and the communication will be hampered.

6. Difference in Perception of a Message: Most of the people perceive a particular situation in different ways. This is mainly because of their perception level are not same or the perception possess by them are different. To overcome this problem, one needs to communicate from different perspectives. And try to verify it from different points of views and then come to a conclusion.

7. Choose of Words: One should be very careful for choosing the words in a business transaction. The application of words such as good, bad, proper, inappropriate and other large number of words can be interpreted in different ways. The practical examples are given below:

A HR Manager handed over a letter to her newly joined Secretary with the instruction," Take it to our stock room and burn it". In the office manager's mind the word "burn" means to make a copy on the company's machine which was operated by a heat process. The secretary thought for a meanwhile that the letter may be important and a photocopy should be preserved. But the secretary was extremely confused and burned the letter with a lighted match and thus destroyed the only copy of this important document.

In another situation a manager tell subordinate to finish the job "as early as possible". The manager expects the subordinate to comply with his instruction immediately but the subordinate may think that the manager wants him to complete the job after his entire assigned job is finished. And thus he may be getting late and his boss is annoyed to him.

Similarly in a business situation, one should be very careful for choosing the words. It can be explained in the following incident.

A private college is running with a course "Bachelor in Optometry & Vision Science" which is basically deals with Eye & Vision Science. During laboratory inspection the inspector who is not from the same background asked the Head of the department, "Sir what is the Optometry status of your teachers?" The Head became confused and meanwhile he realized the fact that the inspector may ask him about the eye condition of his subordinates.

Likewise words such as good, bad, proper, inappropriate and other large number of words can be interpreted in different ways and hence need to use carefully in order to avoid ambiguity.

(B) Non-Verbal Barriers

Non-verbal communication at the workplace is as important as verbal communication as it talks a lot about one's personality and overall individuality. There are certain messages in the organization that need to be conveyed in a non-verbal manner rather than opting for the verbal modes of communication. However, various factors can result in being the barriers to non-verbal communication affecting the business processes and efficiency of the organization.

1. Silence

As it is said 'Silence is Golden' but it can be a very threatening tool and one of the major barriers to non-verbal communication. The lack of expression sends a message itself, which can create a communication barrier between the sender and the receiver. The silence, when not used correctly, can send wrong and misleading signals to the other person raising quite many queries and issues within the team of an organization.

For instance, if the manager is not responding to his subordinate by maintaining silence when the later is giving strategic ideas and inputs, it can indicate as a sign of disregard or disrespect.

2. Body Language

A person's body language can be one of the biggest and most effective tools of communication. But at the same time, it can also be one of the major barriers to non-verbal communication. Factors such as folded hands, lack of eye contact, slouched back, straight face, and not paying attention are those signs of body language that indicate that the person is not interested in the communication.

3. Paralanguage

Paralanguage is the way inflections are used when sending a message verbally. It reflects in the overall attitude of a person, his pitch, tone of voice, and the volume while communicating. Paralanguage creates a nonverbal communication barrier when it is misunderstood or not applied appropriately. If the person seems to be timid or shy while speaking, he comes across as a shy or reserved personality. And such behaviour can affect the other person communicating with him.

4. Facial Expression

Facial expression of a person can also act as the barriers to non-verbal communication. Feelings such as fear, insecurity, jealousy, and others can give away a wrong message or communication to the other person. Facial expressions can be misinterpreted and misunderstood.

For instance, if an employee is discussing some personal issue with his manager but the constant expression on the face of his manager is of the enjoyment or smiling it can indicate that the manger is getting a sadistic pleasure listening to the issues and problems of his team member.

5. Lack of Enthusiasm

When a person lacks enthusiasm whilst fulfilling his roles and responsibilities at his workplace, it indicates that he is low on the aspects of motivation and agility to accomplish the goals and objectives. It affects his speech, body language, and other personality traits resulting in the barriers to non-verbal communication.

6. Emotions

Mental issues such as anxiety, depression, and fear amongst others can act as one of the barriers to non-verbal communication. Any person facing any of these issues is not able and capable to communicate through nonverbal facets of communication.

7. Lack of Focus

Having focus is very important to understand certain aspects of non-verbal communication. But lack of focus during any important meetings or conversations can result in the barriers to non-verbal communication. When the person is unable to catch sign or symbolic language owing to the lack of focus, he won't be able to conduct his tasks and responsibilities in an efficient and effective manner.

8. No Eye Contact

Having a proper eye contact whilst communicating is one the important signs of effective communication but when a person refrains from having eye contact results in the barriers to non-verbal communication affecting the overall flow of the communication.

Conclusion

Barriers to non-verbal communication can, at times, be very tricky and difficult to resolve as they are related to one's emotions and sentiments. But through one to one discussion with the employees and training sessions, there is always a way out.

1.9: Summary

Concept and Meaning of Communication: In this professional world communication skill of a person plays a significant role to decide the career graph and concept. Communication is one of the basic functions of management for any organization.

Purpose of Professional Communication: Providing instruction, integration, evaluation process, giving orders, influences others, projecting image, employee's orientation, and staffing, raising morale.

Features of Successful Professional Communication: It is process which transmits the important ideas, thoughts, plans, feelings etc. Communication skills are considered as an art of techniques of persuasion through the use of verbal and nonverbal features.

Importance of Communication: Communication is indispensable in today's business world. It is said that the world of modern management is the world of communication.

- Helps in smooth running of a business.
- It is a tool of sharing information.
- Develop cooperation and mutual understanding.
- Facilitate employees to perform well.
- Supports manager/(s) to perform better.
- Communication is a tool of coordination.
- Maintaining good human relations.
- Helps to project the image of the enterprise.

Types of Communication: Communication can be classified into verbal, nonverbal, intrapersonal, interpersonal, mass communication and media communication.

Formal Channels of Communications: Formal channel of communication can be segregated into four major channels of communication: Upward, Downward, Horizontal and Diagonal

Barriers to Effective Communication

Verbal Barriers: Verbal barriers are verbal attach, speaking loudly and using complex words.

Improper Encoding: Improper barrier is a frequent barrier in the process of communication.

Semantic or Language Gap: Sometimes the gap arises because much of what people say is subjective or multiple meaning of words or misinterpretation of language.

Variation in Language: Sometimes the words and expression are culture specific. If it is not been used properly it might lead barriers in communication process.

Difference in Perception of a Message: Different people perceive a particular situation in different ways.

Non-verbal Barriers: Various factors can result in being the barriers to non-verbal communication affecting the business processes and efficiency of the organization.

Silence: The silence, when not used correctly, can send wrong and misleading signals to the other person raising quite many queries and issues within the team of an organization.

Body Language: It can be one of the major barriers to non-verbal communication. Factors such as folded hands, lack of eye contact, slouched back, straight face, and not paying attention are those signs of body language that indicate that the person is not interested in the communication.

Paralanguage: Paralanguage creates a nonverbal communication barrier when it is misunderstood or not applied appropriately.

Facial Expression: Facial expression of a person can also act as the barriers to non-verbal communication. Thus facial expression can be misinterpreted and misunderstood.

Lack of Enthusiasm: When a person lacks enthusiasm whilst fulfilling his roles and responsibilities at his workplace, it indicates that he is low on the aspects of motivation and agility to accomplish the goals and objectives. It affects his speech, body language, and other personality traits resulting in the barriers to non-verbal communication.

Emotions: Mental issues such as anxiety, depression, and fear amongst others can act as one of the barriers to non-verbal communication.

Lack of Focus: Lack of focus during any important meetings or conversations can result in the barriers to non-verbal communication.

No Eye Contact: When a person refrains from having eye contact results in the barriers to non-verbal communication affecting the overall flow of the communication.

1.10: Glossary

Body Language: It is the posture of the body. Signs of body language are folded hands, lack of eye contact, slouched back, straight face, and not paying attention.

Diagonal Communication: It is also termed as "Spiral Communication". 'Diagonal Communication' flows in all directions as it has no rigid norms of communication protocol.

Downward Communication: When a communication comes from higher level to the lower level of employees, it called as Downward Communication.

Extra Personal Communication: The communication with non-human entities such as animals, birds etc. is termed as extra personal communication.

Facial Expression: It is basically the expression of a face of by which a person can express his joy, sorrow, fear, anger, etc.

Horizontal Communication: It occurs between peer group or the people working on the same level of an organization.

Improper Encoding: Improper barrier is a frequent barrier in the process of communication.

Intrapersonal Communication: Whenever communication takes places within an individual, it is called 'Intrapersonal Communication'.

Mass Communication: This is mainly the application of tools of mass media.

Media Communication: The main tools for media communication are computers, cell phones, LCD, video, television etc. Presently internet has become very accepted for this communication.

Nonverbal Communication: In this communication, a message is been communicated without using a word.

Non-verbal barriers: Various factors can result in being the barriers to non-verbal communication affecting the business processes and efficiency of the organization.

Oral Communication: In oral communication the sender and the receiver interact face to face.

Paralanguage: It is the way inflections are used when sending a message verbally. It reflects in the overall attitude of a person, his pitch, tone of voice, and the volume while communicating.

Semantic or Language Gap: Sometimes the gap arises because much of what people say is subjective or multiple meaning of words or misinterpretation of language.

Upward Communication: It includes the transmission of information from the subordinates to their seniors.

Variation in Language: Sometimes the words and expression are culture specific. If it is not been used properly it might lead barriers in communication process.

Verbal Barriers: Verbal barriers are verbal attach, speaking loudly and using complex words.

Verbal Communication: A professional person has to deal his /her prime working time in speaking and listening to other person apart from reading and writing.

1.11: Self-Assessment Questions

1. Communication always indicates:

(a) consensus, **(b)** agreement, **(c)** conviction,
(d) understanding

2. Which of the following is NOT a formal channel of communications?

   (a) Upward communication, **(b)** Downward communication, **(c)** Horizontal communication, **(d)** Cross sectional

3. Semantic gap is related with

   (a) language, **(b)** noise, **(c)** attitude, **(d)** dress

4. Communication is best defined as:

(a) Saying what's on your mind, **(b)** venting pent –up feeling, **(c)** sharing opinions, ideas and information, **(d)** exerting verbal authority

5. What do you mean by the term 'communication'? Give reason, why is effective communication vital in today's business world.

6. Effective communication is important in today's business world'? Give justification to your answer.

7. Discuss any four barriers to communication and substantiate your answer with one example for each.

8. What are the main features of successful professional communication?

9. What are the main purposes of communication?

10. "Growth of an organization broadly lies to continuous, multi directional and multilevel flow of communication". Elaborate the statement with examples.

11. Describe how semantic barriers hinder the process of communication?

12. Write short notes on the following:

    (a) Informal Channels of Communication

    (b) Downward Communication

(c) Communication Barriers

(d) Key Elements of Communication

13. Answer the following questions as briefly as possible:

(a) What is Communication?

(b) Mention the Different Types of Communication?

(c) What makes technical communication different from general communication?

14. Discuss any four nonverbal barriers to communication and substantiate your answer with appropriate examples.

Chapter-2
Business Correspondence

Contents

2.0: Learning Objectives

After studying this unit, you will be capable to

- Understand the stages of writing, styles of business correspondences, preparing notes, proof reading;
- Know the way of letter writing;
- Appreciate the essential qualities of a business letter, acknowledgement letter, instruction letter, letter of recommendation, sales letters;
- Learn about memorandum and difference between memos and letter;
- Know the procedure of giving notices and circulars;
- Appreciate the characteristics of CV/Resume, guidelines to prepare CV/Resume and learn the essentials of good resume.

2.1: Stages of Writing

A systematic process has to follow while preparing reports or writing a letter, newsletter, etc. It is essential to follow the process while writing such reports. Naturally it reduces the time spent for developing such documents.

There are no such stringent rules for stages of writing. However, the following stages may help to prepare documents.

1st Step: Generate An Idea

This is an early stage of writing and is considered as critical and complicated stages of writing. Generally it is consists of the following issues:

- What are the implications of the 'Title'?
- What ideas lie behind the 'Title'?
- Ideas to explore
- Ideas has to put on paper
- There should be a mixture of fact/ description/theory / arguments.

2nd Stage: Find Out the Perspective of the Writing

In this stage, a writer has to evaluate the perspective of the writing on the basis of following issues:

- To sort out a complex theme into a clear and logical pattern
- To arrange the sequence in terms of results /output, pro/ anti, before / after, cause /effect, etc.
- To find out the relevance of the topics such as educational /organizational/ societal, etc.
- To find out the basic questions of the topic
- To draw the conceptual frame work

3rd Stage: To Make the Draft

This stage is important for a writer as he/ she has to prepare the draft of the article with utmost care. While preparing the draft, the following things have to bear in mind:

- To prepare the structure of the content
- Plan for sequence of argument
- Plan for paragraph structure
- Plan for go to general to specific

4th Stage: To Write a Draft Version

In this stage, the writer has to be cautious to formulate the draft

- To separate each section on a separate page
- To exclude / include new paragraph

5th Stage: Proof Reading

The final stage is proof reading where it should be done with utmost attentively and vigorously.

2.2: Preparing Notes

Preparing notes is a vital study skill that is essential for various academics and professional purpose. It is a methodical way of writing a text quickly, briefly, and clearly. Thus, preparing notes is a productive skill which integrates both reading as well as writing skills. It involves the following:

a) **Reading Strategy:** A careful reading plan to identify the central idea, the key points, and importing supporting details.

b) **Note Writing Techniques:** This can be broadly divided into three areas:

i) **Copying:** It refers to write precisely what is written.

ii) **Transcribing:** It is writing down verbatim what is said.

iii) **Schematizing:** It is the technique of using graphics to organize notes.

c) **Reduction Devices:** This is unique technique to reduce the expression. This is very useful technique to minimize time and avoid repetition of a word or phrase. Reduction devices are mainly used in 'abbreviations' and 'symbols'.

Use of 'Abbreviations'

There are standard abbreviations used in science and technology.

1. Use of First Letters of the Words: It may be abbreviated by using the first letter. It is applied to abbreviate several English words. The examples are given below:

Word	Abbreviation
East	E
West	W
South	S
North	N
Gram	g
Oxygen	O
Carbon	C
Joule	J

2. Use of First Letters of the Phases: A phase of words may be abbreviated by using the first letters of the words in the phase. The method is applied to abbreviate several English and Latin phases. Some examples are given below:

Word/ Phase	Abbreviation
Cubic Centimeter	cc
With Effect From	w.e.f
Specific Gravity	sg
Per Annum	pm
Curriculum Vitae	cv
Atomic Mass Unit	amu
Take Note That	N.B

3. Use the First Letters of Words/ Phases: A phase or a group of words may be abbreviated by using the first few letters. Examples are given below:

Word/ Phase	**Abbreviation**
Difference	diff
Second	sec
Minute	min
Approximately	approx.
Professor	Prof
Computer	Comp
Subject	sub

4. Use of Symbols: It is required to use appropriate symbols while preparing notes. A few examples are given below:

Symbols	Abbreviation
£	Pound
B	Beta
↓	Downwards arrow
≥	Greater than equal to
©	Copy right
A	Greek small letter alpha
÷	Sign of Division
∞	Infinity
™	Trade mark sign
¥	Yen
±	Plus –Minus sign

5. Special Techniques to Abbreviate: A phase or a group of words are being abbreviated by using some special techniques.

Word/ Phase	Abbreviation
For example	e.g.
that is	i.e.
et cetera, and others	etc.
Compare	cf

6. Use of First Few Letters of Words / Phases: This is very common method of abbreviation. A phase or a group of words may be abbreviated by using the first letter and one or more letters of words/phase.

Word/ Phase	Abbreviation
Month	mth
Hour	hr.
Year	yr.
Magnesium	Mg

2.3: Style of Business Correspondence

The Styles of business letters have changed drastically over the period of time. In the few years back, the style was followed stringently. But,now a day, freedom has been given to the people to follow their own styles. There are still many business houses which use the old layout. However, a good business letter will focus on the subject clearly. A model of business letter is given below:

Fig. 2.1: Model of a Business Letter

XYZ Trading Company
Rashbehari Avenue, Kolkata
Web: www xyztrad.com
Phone (011) 2547325
FAX: (011)2547326

April 2, 2019
Mr. Hari Kumar
Sales Manager
Excel Computers,
Ajmer Road, Jaipur-3020006

Dear Mr. Kumar,

Please refer to your advertisement in March 28, issue of the Telegraph (Kolkata edition) about the HP scan Jet 4200B scanner

Our company is interested in buying 50 (Fifty) scanners for our corporate office. We would be glad if you could send us the necessary information about the product.

- Product Specification
- Special Features of HP Scan Jet 4200B Scanner
- An Estimate for the Cost of Fifty Units
- Amount of Corporate Discount
- Terms & Condition of Purchase
- Delivery Date from Placing the Order

Looking forward for your reply

Sincerely

Chiranjib Maitra

Purchase Manager

2.4: Using Simple Words

The main objective of communication is to transmit the message to others. So, for the effective communication, the sender must determine the purpose of communication using simple and understandable words.

Since the words chosen must have the same meaning in the minds of both the writer and the reader for successful communication, guidelines on the preferred word choice are very important

The examples are given below:

Rather than words, which are	Use words which are
General	specific
Complex	simple
Passive	active
Negative	positive
Rather than words, which are	Use words which are
Long	short
unfamiliar	familiar
Unnecessary	necessary
Formal	conversational

It is also necessary for the sender to choose the words and use of proper verbs and use of words /phase which is concrete, specific, simple, active, short, and concise. It is also recommended that for effective communication, the complex words have to be replaced with the simple words. The examples are given below:

- Endeavor (try)
- Initiate (start)
- Modification (change)

- Termination (end)
- Utilize (use or employ)
- Indispensable(vital)

2.5: Proof Reading

Proof reading is not an ability of a person. Rather, it is an assimilated skill. Proof reading does not mean simply skimming through the writing on the last time. It means revising the earlier one to make it better. In proof reading, the corrections in grammar, spelling, and punctuation has to be done carefully.

Proof reading is not just about errors. There is a few scope of proof reading.

- It polishes the sentences at this point,
- Making them interesting and smooth,
- Use of direct sentence,
- Eliminate the unnecessary phases,
- Avoid repetition of words.

2.6: Letter Writing

Business correspondence is a vital instrument of decision making in the modern business world. The significance of business correspondence has increased. In fact, this is a vital channel of communication. In order to succeed in today's competitive environment, it is required to adopt effective letter writing skills. The business letter may be of varies types like -a letter to request for services, request for action, inviting quotations, sending quotations, placing orders, inviting tenders, sales letters, claim and adjustment letters, social correspondence, etc.

2.7: Essential Components of a Business Letter

The success of a business letter depends upon effective communication of the message to achieve its main purpose. The following are the essentials of business letter:

1. Clearness and Clarity: Every letter should clearly convey the message. The sender should keep into mind the level of understanding of the receiver. Words and phrases should be chosen appropriately. To write an effective business letter, simple language is required and long sentence should be avoided.

2. Completeness: A business letter should contain all the necessary information. It is needed to put in the letter all the necessary reference no. and dates of the earlier correspondence.

3. Conciseness: A business letter should always be concise or brief. In the modern business world time is precious and should not be wasted in pointless and irrelevant statements in a letter.

4. Sincerity: A business letter should be written sincerely. Business letter should never contain any false or suppress information. The sender is expected to be sincere in giving information and making statement of facts.

5. Simplicity: A business letter should be simple, clear, and understandable.

2.8: Acknowledgement Letter: This is used when the sender acknowledges someone for the support. An acknowledgement letter speaks volumes about the gratitude that the sender received earlier. Thus, this type of letter is used to thank to someone.

An example of this type of letter follows:

Fig: 2.2 Model of an Acknowledgement Letter

Gouri Group of Industries
4/2 Millan Palli, Durgapur, West Bengal
Phone: 0343 2533881-84
Fax 0343-2533991

GPT/T/40
21 March, 2018

Ms. Baisakhi Mitra
Event Manager
BF 162, Salt Lake, Sector-I
Kolkata- 713264

Dear Ms. Mitra,

We would like to appreciate the commitment, support, and cooperation we received from you in organizing two days workshops on Advertising: Possibilities and Perspectives from 22-24 February, 2018 in Durgapur, West Bengal. Throughout the event, your suggestions and advice helped us to organize the workshop in a systematic and methodical way. Everybody appreciated your commitment, positive attitude, and professionalism with which you have managed the event

We look forward to be associated with you in future.

Thanks and regards

Yours sincerely

Dr. D. Banerjee

Convener

2.9: Instruction Letter

A letter of instruction is a simple routine letter that consists of directions for the receiver. It consists of three parts.

i) Opening: Purpose of instruction

ii) Body: Details

iii) Closing: Focus on action

A sample of Instruction letter is given below:

Fig 2.3: Model of an Instruction Letter

March 21, 2014

Mr. Partha Chatterjee

Chief Manager, State Bank of India

Durgapur Main Branch

Durgapur

Dear Mr. Chatterjee,

I would like to draw your kind attention that I have lost my cheque book number 2343809. Please issue me a new cheque book. Also stop any payment against any cheque bearing the number 2343801 to 2343850.

I have signed the cheque requisition slip and handed over the same to my office peon. I am sending him to collect the cheque book. I shall be obliged, if you can give him the cheque book.

Thanking you.

Sincerely,

Dr. D. Banerjee

Managing Director

Gouri Group of Industries, Durgapur, West Bengal

2.10: Letter of Recommendation

The letter is being written to recommend a person for a job position or admission for higher studies. The letter simply states the positive aspects of the applicant's personality, required skills.

Sometimes, a letter of recommendation is even used for promoting a person in a company. An example of this type of letter is given below:

Fig 2.4: Model of a Letter of Recommendation

To,

The General Manager-HR

Maya Industries Limited

Salt lake

Kolkata-19

Date: 12.09.19

Dear Sir,

I must give you 'thanks' for your letter dated 21st March, 2014. I welcome the opportunity to support Ms. Aparna Bose's application for the post of Assistant Marketing Officer in your organization.

Ms. Aparna Bose has been one of the most diligent and talented students of our college. Though her DGPA (9.2) itself speaks highly of her academic excellence. Besides doing well in studies Ms. Bose has successfully developed herself as a versatile and multifaceted individual during her stay on the campus. Besides this, she also has displayed her leadership qualities from time to time.

In the above aspects, I find Ms. Bose's positive attitude and sense of commitment. It gives me pleasure to recommend her to work for your organization.

Yours sincerely

Dr. Abir Mitra

Principal, Management Studies

Excellent Academy, Kolkata

2.11: Sales Letter

Sales letter is essential to communicate with the client/ customer. There are some specific guidelines to write the same

- To draw the attention in an attractive manner
- Interest building about the product
- Benefit of the product purchase
- Induce the customer/ client to take necessary steps
- Close with a clincher sentence

Fig 2.5: Model of a Sales Letter

To

Mr. Partha Chatterjee
Regional Manager-Marketing & Sales
ABC Limited
BA 178 Salt Lake
Kolkata-64

Date: 2nd September, 2019

Dear Sir,

Greetings from Gouri Group of Industries!!

Winter is round the corner. You must be thinking how you keep your office warm so that the employee of your organization feels comfortable at work place. We have an excellent solution of it. Considering the need, we have produced room heaters of different capacities. The enclosed pamphlet gives their detailed specifications.

You are requested to fill the requisition and sent herewith and mail. Person from our company will call you and give a demo for the location of room heaters so that your entire office remains warm and comfortable. This technical assistance is free of cost.We also may add that each room heater is guaranteed for three years against all manufacturing defects. If you want to place your order before 30th October, 2019, a special discount will be offered.

Hope and pray for a favorable disposal from your end.

Yours faithfully

Sridip Banerjee

Zonal Head-Marketing

XYZ Limited

Mumbai

2.12: Appreciation Letter

Everybody feels good when he /she are appreciated for their achievements. Keeping in view, the impact of appreciation letter is written in the organization. Generally this type of letter is written by a superior to his/her junior. An organization also writes an appreciation letter to other organization, thanking the client for doing business with them. This kind of letter is obviously helpful in strengthening the bonding between two individuals or organizations.

Fig: 2.6: Model of an Appreciation Letter

To Date: 12th January, 2020

Mr. Partha Chatterjee

Computer Teacher

DAV Model School, Durgapur

Sub: letter to appreciate your contribution in the project: "TechCHAI".

Dear Mr. Chatterjee,

I would like to appreciate all the hard work and digital efforts that you put into completing the project "TechCHAI". It was absolutely your hard work and research that has ultimately given us a notable result. We also feel proud that your project has been appreciated by the Government of India and Government of Moscow. On behalf of all the members of Governing body of DAV, I would like to thank you for your outstanding achievements. We are grateful to have you as one of the team leaders in this project.

Your dedication to work, desire to experiment and find new ways to achieve goals, out of the box thinking and personal involvement is outstanding. Moreover, you have added a fame to become an Indian delegate to this project and completed successfully.

We are grateful to have you as a member of our school and we hope to see you grow in this organization.

Thanking You

With Regards

Dr. P. Dey

Principal

DAV Model School, Durgapur

2.13: Apology Letter

In the professional world, an apology letter is written for a failure in delivering the desired results. This letter is also written if someone happens to have inflicted undue or undesirable inconvenience to somebody. This type of letter helps in patching and saving the writer from spoiling the relation. A sincere apology can go a long way towards winning back a professional linkage.

Fig: 2.7: Model of an Apology Letter

Date: 12th January, 2020

Abir Chatterjee

Country Manager: Silicon Limited

24 East 32nd Place

Bangalore. India

Contact: +91 876xxxxxxxxxxx

E mail: sixxxxx@gmail.com

Dear Mr. S. Sandiliyan,

On behalf of my company, I would like to apologize for the unhappy experience has had with my team. We deeply regret the way your request was handled. We would like to take full responsibility for the mistake and assure you that we are taking necessary steps to prevent it from happening in future. Thank you for bringing the issue to our attention.

We value our customers and would request you to freely provide feedback about our services. If you have any further quarries or would like to discuss regarding this matter, please feel free to contact me at my cell number. We look forward to continue our service to you as a valued customer.

Thank you once again for your invaluable support and feed back

Thanks & Regards

Abir Mitra

(Country Manager: Silicon Limited)

2.14: Composing Business Messages

The planning and composing process for developing the various types of business messages are almost same. While composing business message, three things are essential.

1. Determine the business purpose
2. Analyze the receiver(s) for the 'you' view point
3. Compose the content of the message

It is essential to control the vocabulary level of the business message so that it is understandable for the receiver. In addition to that it is important to check the ethical and legal part of the message.

2.15: Memorandum

A memorandum (memo) is the most commonly used of communication within an organization. A memorandum letter is a letter comprising a statement that is usually written by higher authorities of an organization. In establishments and offices, memos are used to circulate the information to the employees regarding the happenings in the company. Memos are generally less formal than a letter.

While writing a memo, the following things should be followed:

- To write a memorandum in a brief and simple way.
- Memos do not exceed a paragraph or two and is usually just bulleted list of information.
- To maintain a professional tone and easy to understand language.
- It should not include any personal statements.

The following elements usually constitute the structure of a memo:

i) Name of the Organization

ii) Name /Designation of the Receiver

iii) Name and Designation of the Sender

iv) Reference

v) Date

vi) Subject

vii) Body

viii) The signature of the sender

Fig 2.8: Model of a Memo

Maya Industries Limited

Inter Office Memorandum

To: Managing Director
From: Sales Manager
Ref: BITT/179

Date: 21March, 2018

Subject: National Conference on Sales Promotion

As directed by the authority, I have attended the National Conference held in Kolkata on 18 and 19 March 2018 and presented a paper on the strategies for the promotion of sales of washing machines.

There was in depth discussion of various methods of capturing market through advertisements on electronic and print media. It was comprehended that these media had a major impact on sales promotion. However, keeping in view the competitive edge, it is necessary to devise and use other ways of reaching the customer across the country. Some suggestive measures have been put forward like: door to door visit, demonstration at strategic points of different parts of the town, paper inserts, distribution of handbills in regional language, display of danglers, and hoardings.

I am enclosing the details of the suggestions made at the conference. However, it would be better to conduct a market survey before devising new methods of promoting the sale of our machines.

D. Banerjee
Zonal Manager

2.16: Difference between Memos and Letter

Memos and letters are the two most common types of business communications. Memos resemble letters in that they communicate information and are commonly used in modern business world. However, memos differ from letters in several ways:

- Memos are used within an organization. Business letter is given to other organization.
- Memos have direct style, but business letter comprise of different styles.
- Memos do not have any salutation while in letter salutation is essential.
- Memos do not have any complementary closing. Business letter have a complementary closing.
- Memos have a specific format that is very different from a business letter.

2.17: Notices

A notice can be posted on notice boards by various departments of an organization. Notices can be used to inform people about the wide variety of topics e.g. social occasions, notification of meeting, etc. A notice must be eye catching, clear and concise, and should contain only relevant information. An ideal notice is given below

Fig 2.9: Model of a Notice

NOTICE

MAKAUT Odd Semester Examinations, Form Fill up Session (for 3rd /5th /7th Semester)

Attn: All students under MAKAUT (UG&PG)

The eligible students of MAKAUT those have cleared their fees and have fulfilled attendance criteria are hereby directed to deposit examination fee of Rs.1,000 and Rs 800/- (for Backlog) against the Odd Semester Examination, 2016.

All the above concerned students are directed to submit the examination fee to the Accounts Department (batch wise) with the fees challan written thereon the students name, course, semester, and university Roll no.

The schedule is given below: Submission of Fees for Backlog Paper/(s): from 22.11.16 to 24.11.16 (11.00am-1.30pm) (All semester)

Submission of Fees for Regular: from 22.11.16 to 24.11.16 (11.00am-1.30pm) (All semester)

After submission of the fees to the Accounts Department, the students are advised to follow the process flow:

1. Take a printout of Regular Examination form and submit the same to the respective Class Teacher/Mentor along with the money receipt marked as " Exam Cell"
2. Rs 1,000/- &Rs 500/- banned currency by the Government will not be accepted.

Dr. D. Mitra
Head of the Department
Examinations & University Affairs
ABC Knowledge Campus, Kolkata

Copy to:

1. Principal (NBS/ NSOHM/)(necessary direction to the concern team members pl)_
2. Dear Academics-NCMT/NBS
3. Account's Dept.
4. HODs/In charge (NCMT,NFET& NSHOM)
5. Student's Notice Board (BHMCT/ NBS/NCMT /B-TECH)
6. Hostel Superintendent (Pl arrange to display in Hostel Notice Board)
7. Staff Notice Board
8. Manager ITES

2.18: Circular

Office circular is formal in nature is meant to bring the notice of a certain audience matters of importance to the organization. They are broadly used to circulate information like change in working days/hours, inviting applications from employees for promotion or seeking suggestions on certain issues related to the organization. They are usually brief, precise, and persuasive pieces of writing brought to the notice of staff.

Fig 2.10: Model of a Circular

Date: 27.05.19

CDE Knowledge Campus, Kolkata

This is to inform all the team members of CDE Kolkata Campus that for smooth operation of University Exam. 2019 no leave will be sanctioned by the concerned departmental head except medical exigencies.

Our campus will remain open on 01.06.19 (Sat), 02.06.19(Sun), 08.06.19(Sat) & 15.06.19 (Sat) as per the directives of the Controller of Examinations MAKAUT due to University Examinations.

D. Roy

CDE Knowledge Campus, Kolkata (CEO& Director)

2.19: Agenda

An agenda clearly sets out the matters to be discussed at a meeting. It should be notified to the participants in advance of a meeting so the members can present the relevant information in the meeting. It helps in conducting the meeting in proper order and reduces irrelevant discussions. A properly produced agenda also ensures that the meeting is conducted efficiently and follows a logical order, which is accepted by all the participants. The items of the agenda are arranged in increasing order of importance and each item bears a number.

The following information is required to serve an agenda:

i) Name of the Organization

ii) Date of Circulation

iii) Day, Date, Time, and Venue of Meeting

iv) Signature of the Convener of the Meeting

In some cases, the following items might be included in agenda.

- Minutes of the Previous Meeting
- Suggestions Received from the Members
- Actions Taken

2.20: Minutes

Minutes are taken during each formal meeting. They are formal written record of what was discussed and of decisions made during the meeting. The style of minutes is impersonal, objective, and matter-of -fact. Minutes follow the pattern of agenda and bear the same numbers. For each item, a heading is given and the discussion / decision on it is recorded. Keeping minutes of the meetings is a legal requirement of public and private sector companies.

As minutes are self-sufficient records; it is necessary to put the following details:

i) Name of the organization

ii) Day, date, time, and venue of the meeting

iii) Name of the Chairman or the person presiding the meeting

iv) Names of the members present

v) Names of members absent

vi) Record of discussions -item wise

vii) Signature of the chairman/ convener of the meeting

Fig 2.11: Model of the Minutes

Minutes

Gouri Industries Limited, Kolkata

Minutes of the Sixteenth Annual General Body Meeting of the company held at 14 hours on Tuesday 12th March,2012 at 2/14 Rowland Road, Kolkata.

Members Present:

Smt. Gouri Chatterjee - Chairman

Sri. Partha Chatterjee -Director

Sri. Argha Bose- Director

Sri. Sayantan Ghosh- Director

In attendance: Sri. Rohit Dhillon- Secretary

Sl. No	Agenda	Minutes
1.01	Confirmation of the minutes of the last meeting	The minutes of the meeting held on 12 March, 2012 were approved and signed by the Chairman.
1.02	Directors' Report and Annual Accounts	Directors' Report and Annual Accounts circulated there-with were taken as read. The Chairman reported the progress of the company and highlighted its achievements besides outlining the next year's development plan. On a motion by Sri. Rohit Dhillon-Secretary, the Directors' Report and Annual Accounts as audited by the company auditors were approved and adopted.

1.03	Auditors' Report	The Auditors Report which had already been circulated was taken as read and approved. It was noted that the assets of the company had increased by Rupees 80 lac.
1.04	Appointment of Auditors	On a motion by Sri. Partha Chatterjee, seconded by Mr. Punit Sharma, it was resolved that Ms. Asoke Sahaika be reappointed as auditors of the company for the next accounting year at a fee of Rs. 60,500/-
1.05	Declaration of Dividend	On a motion by Sri. Argha Bose and seconded by Mr. Pallab Ghost, it was adopted: 'That a dividend of Rs.50 per equity share ,subject to the deduction of income tax, as recommended by the Board of Directors is approved and will be paid to the shareholders whose names stood on the books of the company on 1 March 2012'.
1.06	Election of the Directors	Sri. D. Thakur proposed that the retiring Director Sri. Sayantan Ghosh be reappointed. The following resolution moved by him and seconded by Sri. Basu Chatterjee was adopted' resolved that Sri. Sayantan Ghosh, being eligible for reelection and hereby reelected

		as Director of the company for the period of next two years.
1.07	Next Year's Development Plan	The suggestion of a shareholder, Sri. Dip Dutta that the main points of next year's development plan of the Company be printed and circulated to shareholders was admitted by the chair and adopted by the general body.

The meeting ended with a vote of thanks to the chairman.

Gouri Chatterjee
Chairman

Rohit Dhillon
Secretary

2.21: Preparing the Resume / CV

There is no specific design for resume. The design of a resume largely depends on a person's back round, employment needs, career goals, and professional conventions in the area of specialization. For best results a resume must be designed to reflect the candidate's personality.

However, while preparing a resume, the following answer should be reflected.

a) How can the employer contact the candidate?

b) What are his/her career objectives?

c) Which institute/ college/university have been attended?

d) Which courses (academic/ professional) has been attended?

e) What is his/her work experience?

f) What are his / her career achievements?

g) What are his/her special skills?

h) What are the awards/ honors he/she has received?

i) What are his/her special interest/hobbies

2.22: Characteristics of a Good Resume

The main features of a good resume are as follows:

- Use of simple and clean structure
- Symmetrical and balanced
- Focused
- There should be a consistency in the use of italics, capital letters, bullets, boldface.
- There are absolutely no errors.
- All the basic information is to be included.
- Jobs listed include a title, the name of the organization, and the years.
- Strengths are to be highlighted.

Fig 2.12: Format of a Model CV

CURRICULUM VITAE

Name of the candidate ______________________

Contact Address E-Mail

Contact No.

CAREER PROFILE

Objective

EXPERIENCE

Administrative

Academic

ACADEMIC

Degree	University	Year	Stream	Class /Div

PAPER PUBLICATIONS

Selected Publications :

TRAINING & WORKSHOP

Primary Training & Workshop

FDP

CONFERENCE & SEMINAR

Paper Presented in Conference

COMPUTER KNOWLEDGE

RESEARCH & PROJECTS

AWARD & RECOGNITION

Award & Recognition

HOBBIES & LEISURE

Hobbies

PERSONAL DETAILS

Date of Birth

Languages Known

Marital Status

I do hereby declare that the above information is correct to the best of my knowledge and belief.

Name with signature of the candidate

2.21: Summary

A systematic process has to follow while preparing reports or writing a letter. There are five stages which may help to prepare documents. Preparing notes is a productive skill which improves the reading and writing skills. It is important to know the use of 'Abbreviations'. It is also necessary to know the style of Business letter, Acknowledgement letter, Appreciation letter, Apology letter, Instruction letter, Sales letter. Composing of business messages plays an important role in modern business world. A memorandum (memo) is the most commonly use of communication within an organization. It is used to circulate the information to the employees regarding the happenings in the company. There is specific structure to write the memo. In this context, it is relevant to understand the difference between memos and letters. The notice and circulars are very often circulated from office. The proper structure of these should be followed. The agenda and minutes of the meeting are to be maintained by the public and private sector companies. The design of a Curriculum Vitae (CV) is largely depends on a person's back round, employment needs, career goals, and professional conventions in the area of specialization. For best results a resume must be designed to reflect the candidate's personality. Hence, it is deemed necessary to know to prepare the appropriate CV.

2.20: Glossary

Circular: Office circular is formal in nature is meant to bring the notice of a certain audience matters of importance to the organization.

Copying: It refers to write precisely what is written.

Curriculum Vitae: Curriculum Vitae is the reflection of the candidate's personality. There is no specific design for resume. The design of a resume largely depends on a person's back round, employment needs, career goals, and professional conventions in the area of specialization.

Memorandum: A memorandum (memo) is the most commonly use of communication within an organization. In establishments and offices, memos are used to circulate the information to the employees regarding the happenings in the company.

Notes: Preparing notes is a vital study skill that is essential for various academics and professional purpose. It is a methodical way of writing a text quickly, briefly, and clearly.

Proof Reading: It means revising the earlier one to make it better. In proof reading, the corrections in grammar, spelling, and punctuation has to be done carefully.

Reduction Devices: This is unique technique to reduce the expression. Reduction devices are mainly used in 'Abbreviations' and 'Symbols'.

Schematizing: It is the technique of using graphics to organize notes.

Transcribing: It is writing down verbatim what is said.

2.21: Self-Assessment Questions

1. What is the main purpose of business writing?
2. What are the main stages of writing a document?

3. Why proof reading is important? What are the various things one should look for while proof reading
4. What are the main stages of writing?
5. Write short notes on :
    a) Note Writing Techniques
    b) Reduction devices
    c) Objectives of business letter
6. What is the importance of formal and style in business writing?
7. 'There is a few scope of proof reading'- Elaborate your views.
8. Give two examples for the following :
    a) Use of first letters of the words
    b) Use the first letters of words/ phases
    c) Use of symbols
9. What are the essential qualities of a business letter?
10. What are the things are essential for developing effective business message?
11. 'Business letter is a silent ambassador of goodwill'. Explain the statement.
12. What are memo? What purpose do they serve? Why it is important to learn to write memos?
13. What is the general format of memo? Offer general guidelines for writing good business memos.
14. What are the main characteristics of a good resume?

Exercises

15. Assume that the head of the department you have received a request for writing a recommendation letter for a former student of yours who intend to pursue his post graduate

degree from a university. Your recommendation letter should highlight the student's strength achievements and sustainability of the course he intends to pursue.

16. Assuming that your organization has recently conducted a week long training programme for newly recruited junior level managers. The training programme was aimed at improving the communication and interpersonal skills of the young personnel. Assuming yourself to be the co-coordinator of the programme draft a letter of acknowledgement appreciating the cooperation received from the resource persons during the programme.

17. Imagine yourself to be the Sales Manager of Hi Tech Solutions limited, Kolkata; your company has recently launched a new low cost laptop 003 CP in the market. In order to promote the sale of this model, draft a sales letter to be sent to colleges, universities, and other organizations.

18. Imagine yourself an Administrative officer of XYZ Co. Ltd., you want to conduct a Seminar. Design a notice for circulation to all team members

19. Imagine that you are the Secretary in attendance at the fifth annual meeting of the Executive Committee of the Maya Industries Ltd. held at 4 pm on Tuesday, 6March, 2014. Write a minutes of meeting assuming the agenda to be as follows:

1.01: Minutes of the previous meeting

1.02: Chairman's report

1.03: Appointment of an auditor for the next year

1.04: Purchase of Assets

1.05: Revision of DA to the employees

1.06: Other relevant matter with the permission of the chair

Chapter-3

Report Writing

Contents

3.0: Learning Objectives

After studying this unit, you will be capable to

- Understand the meaning ,objectives, and types of report;
- Differentiate various formats of report;
- Comprehend the steps in report writing;
- Learn the essentials of good report.

3.1: Meaning of Report

A report is a narrative description of an event which is provided to someone who was absent at the time of occurrence. It is an organized statement of information concerning to a particular subject matter which is prepared after an investigation and provided to the concerned stakeholders. Report can be written or oral. Mainly, it is in the written form. Some definitions of report are mentioned below:

According to R. C. Sharma and Krishna Mohan, "A report is a formal communication written for a specific purpose that includes a description of procedures followed for collection and analysis of data, their significance, the conclusions drawn from them and the recommendations, if required."

Ober said, "A report is an orderly and objective presentation of information that assists in decision making and problem solving."

According to Betty and Kay, "A Report is a written or oral message presenting information that will help a decision maker to solve a business problem."

From this discussion, we can state that report may be written or oral statement of truth connecting to a specific event. It is a significant document that assists in decision making.

3.2: Objectives of Preparing Report

The main important intention of a report is to provide information regarding any event to the appropriate authority. It assists mangers to take correct and realistic decisions. The objectives of a report may be stated as under:

1. Means of Communication: A report is very useful document for upward communication. A report is made and provided to appropriate authority who requires that information for taking a variety of decisions.

2. Satisfy Interested Parties: The concerned parties of report are top rank executives, Government agencies, shareholders, creditors, clients, and public community. Diverse kinds of reports are made to persuade the requirements of concerned stakeholders.

3. Serve as a Record: Reports give precious and significant records for future reference. These provide a very rich source of information for future reference.

4. Legal Requirements: A few reports are prepared to fulfil the legal necessities. For example, annual reports of companies are made and supplied the same to the shareholders of the company as per the Companies Act, 1956.

5. Develop Public Relations: General progress report of business and deployment of national resources are also prepared and provided before the public. It enhances the goodwill of a business and fosters public relations.

6. Basis to Measure Performance: Individual performance report is made to take promotional or incentive decision. Group or departmental performance is also made for the disbursement of bonus.

7. Control: Reports are the foundation of controlling. Several actions of improvement are usually taken on the basis of reports. It helps to develop the performance of employees in an organization.

3.3: Types of Report

It is difficult to clearly define and demarcate the categories of business reports. There are several kinds of business reports which may be grouped as under:

1. On the Basis of Legal Requirement

On the above basis, the business reports may be statutory or non-statutory.

a) Statutory Report: Statutory reports are made in order to accomplish the legal compliance. Under Companies Act, Statutory

Report is made in the prescribed form after holding statutory meeting within the period of six months after the incorporation. In addition to this, Annual Report, Auditor's Report, Report by Inspector appointed to investigate into company's affairs, are Statutory Reports.

b) Non Statutory Report: Non-statutory reports are made not because of legal compulsion but because of necessity.

These reports are made: **(i)** for the managerial and other amenities,**(ii)** for taking judgment in a matter,**(iii)** for formulating policy,**(iv)** for predicting the future or **(v)**for efficient and effective functioning.

2. On the Basis of Formality

On this modus operandi, reports may be formal or informal. Formal reports are made as per the formal structure and established rules. Informal reports do not require the formal structure.

a) Formal Report

Formal reports are made as per the formal structure and established rules and presented before the appropriate authority. Reports made by officials or committees under constituted bodies like Companies, Cooperative Societies, Local Bodies, etc. are usually known as formal report.

b) Informal Report

Informal report is made as per the ease of the reporter and presented before the person as per the requirement. An informal report is given either in the form of letter or memorandum.

3. On the Basis of Frequency

On this basis, reports may be routine or special reports. Routine reports are reports structured and submitted at usual intervals. In contrast, special reports are concerned with single or special situation.

a) Routine Report

This report is made and presented to the director at particular intervals. This report contains detailed statement of facts without giving any view or suggestion of the reporter. Some examples are Report of Directors to the Annual General Meeting (AGM), Auditor's Report to the AGM, Sales Report, Production Report, and the like.

b) Special Report

This report is made and presented to the top level executives on specific demand. It generally contains the views or suggestions of the reporter. Some examples are opening of a new branch, introducing a novel produce in the market, improving the quality, and the like.

4. On the Basis of Functions

On this basis, business reports may be informational or analytical reports.

a) Informational Report

The Informational Reports only present the facts along with summary without analyzing, interpreting, and making recommendations. Examples of such report are Progress Reports, Sales Reports, Production Report, etc.

b) Analytical Report

An analytical report contains the facts, views, opinions of reporters, and others and includes the causes for an issue or an event and required remedial action with recommendations.

5. On the Basis of Subject Matter

On this basis, business reports may be problem solving report, fact-finding report, performance report, technical report, etc.

a) Problem Solving Report

A problem may arise in any department or in the entire organization. Hence, the top level management may seek a report for solving the problem. The reporter collects various information to find the causes for such problem. Moreover, this report is completed with the ways of solving the problem. This report is called Problem Solving Report.

b) Fact Finding Report

A machine may be collapsed in the factory location. Sometimes, there may be a struggle between the two groups of workers. Now, the management wants to get the actual reason for break down and clash between the two groups. In this situation, the reporter analyses these happenings through exhaustive investigation and reveals the truth. At last, the reporter provides the fact finding report to the top level executive.

c) Performance Report

The business organization desires to get the performance of every department periodically or performance of a branch or performance of newly appointed employee or performance of existing employees for promotion, transfer, and the like. The management is not in a position to take any decision without knowing the performance. Hence, a reporter is asked to prepare the performance report.

d) Technical Report

There is lot of changes made in the technology. Whenever a company introduces mechanical process instead of manual process, the level of technology required is to be assessed. Sometimes, a design may be changed in the existing product, if so, latest technology should be adopted. In this case, a full report is essential to top management for taking a decision. This report is called Technical Report.

6. On the Basis of Writers

On this basis, business reports may be Individual Reports and Committee Reports.

a) Individual Report

Reports presented by Branch Manager, Personnel Manager, Marketing Manager, the Company Secretary, etc., are individual reports. These reports are related to their own departments.

b) Committee Report

In many times, reports are necessary on subjects involving many departments. In these circumstances, committees are usually formed to prepare reports. These reports are made after a careful deliberation of the members.

3.4: Format of Report

Report can be organized in three ways. These are as follows:

1. **Letter form**
2. **Memorandum form**
3. **Letter text combination form**

1. Letter Form

This form is followed in case of concise and casual reports. Its major components are as follows:

1. Heading;
2. Date;
3. Address;
4. Salutation;
5. Body;
6. Complementary close;
7. Signature.

The body of the letter can be separated into the following divisions:

- **Introduction:** In this section, the writer indicates the problem.
- **Findings:** In this section, the major results of the investigation are exhibited.
- **Recommendations**: Recommendations are put in the final section of the body.

The sample is given below to give an idea about the structure.

Example of Report in Letter Form

Senco Gold Ltd.

(A house for best Garments)

Esplanade, Kolkata

25th May, 2020

Managing Director

Senco Gold Ltd.

Esplanade, Kolkata

Ref: Negligence of duty by the staff in our Durgapur Showroom

Dear Sir,

As per your instruction, I visited our Durgapur showroom to inspect its functioning. I am submitting my report hereunder after investigation.

A number of valuable customers bought some fashionable garments but faced a number of problems for appropriate fitting after purchase. They tried to return the garments but failed because there was no assistant to receive the complaint. Consequently, they informed to our complaint department and filed complaints about this issue.

In our Durgapur branch, there is only one attendant named Mr. Saikat who is responsible to handle the after sales service. He has been found to be very irregular for the previous three (3) months. Accordingly, our customers are dissatisfied causing a decline in our sales.

Therefore, I do not have any hesitation to suggest that Mr. Saikat may be served a notice and an efficient staff may be deployed instead of him.

I expect that a fast action will be taken based on my suggestion for the sake of our company.

Yours faithfully,

Nirmal Chandra Roy

2. Memorandum Form

It is an easy method of presenting the report. Here, the strict rules and regulations are not maintained. The date is written at the top, followed by the receiver's name, writer's name, and the subject matter of the report. Next follows the real text as well as the conclusion.

A Sample of Memorandum Form

25th May, 2020

To: Mr. Subhajit Pahari

From: Nirmal Chandra Roy

Subject: Decrease in sales in the month of March, 2020

Here is the report you sought concerning to the reduction in sales in the month of March 2020. Our product even though reached in time in the market but the price was higher than that of similar competitive products. Consequently, our objective for selling 40,000 units failed.

I would like to recommend the rapid reduction of our product price.

Nirmal Chandra Roy

Executive, Sales

3. Letter Text Combination Form

Long and formal reports are written in this form. This form includes three (3) major parts:

A. Introductory parts

B. The body of the report

C. Appended parts

The complete part of such report is as follows:

A. Introductory Parts

1. Title Page: Under the title page, title of the report, the reader's as well as reporter's name and submission date are mentioned.

2. Authorization Letter: After the title page, authorization letter is attached. Such letter generally mentions the objectives, research area, time and cost, submission date, and any other directions.

3. Letter of Transmittal: Such letter contains the submission date of a report, the name as well as the position of the report writer, an outline of the report, a request for reader's comments and suggestion.

4. Acknowledgments: This section acknowledges the person or organizations from which guidance and assistance were taken to make the report.

5. Table of Contents: This table acts as a road map of the report for the reader. It helps to search any particular topic.

6. List of Illustrations and Graphs: If the report contains a lot of illustrations and graphs then respective page number and title are to be provided.

7. Executive Summary or Abstract: An abstract is a synopsis of a report. It tells the reader about the report. It specifies the important parts of the total report. Consequently, busy executives can save time as there is no need to go through the every page of the report.

B. The Body of the Report

1. Introduction: It is the initial part of the body of the report. This part informs the reader about the problem at hand. This part includes: Authorization for the report, need and rationale of the report, span of the study with a lucid description of the limitation, problem statement, developing hypothesis, methodology to resolve the problem, meaning of particular terms and symbols.

2. Description: This section of the report provides all the collected information. The main objective of this section is to present data in a structured form. It may include charts, graphs, and statistical tables with suitable explanations.

3. Conclusions: In the section, the main findings are assessed. Any conclusions presented should be fair and unbiased, and should not contain the writer's own opinions.

4. Recommendations: These are the writer's own opinions on the basis of conclusions of the report. Recommendations have to be realistic, i.e. it should be based on the facts enclosed in the report.

C. Appended Parts

1. List of References: This section contains the total record of secondary sources used in the report. This list can be given alphabetically or chronologically.

2. Bibliography: This is a list of books and journals which are taken into consideration prior to or during the preparation of a report.

3. Glossary: A glossary is a list of a number of technical or special words with their proper explanations. These words may be given in the beginning or the end. It should be decided by the reporter.

4. Appendix: There are times when large amounts of data or statistics cannot be easily inserted into the main findings. Therefore, this information can be given in an appendix at the end of the report. Statistical data, charts, and diagrams that are not generally included in the main body of the report are mentioned here.

5. Index: This is an alphabetical list of subjects of the report. An index assists the reader to trace any topic simply and quickly.

3.5: Steps of Report Writing

The following five steps are suggested in preparing a report.

1. Investigating the Source of Information: Investigating the information source is a kind of groundwork. It is to be done right in the beginning. The extent of investigation will be decided on the length and significance of the report. Most significant sources of information are: company files, personal observation, interviews, questionnaires, etc.

2. Taking Notes: In the course of investigations, the writer takes various important notes related to the subject. Then there is no time to analyse them and determine how they will be of help in the final report. But as the writer deeps turning them in his mind repeatedly, a kind of patter starts emerging and he begins to be aware about what is relevant and what is not. It is a general type of pattern but it gives the writer at least a starting point.

3. Analysing the Data: Now is the time to analyse the collected data in the context of the pattern that has evolved. Lots of data will have to be rejected while a need might be felt to collect more data. The final pattern will emerge at this stage. The writer should not be hurry in this stage, since this is the most vital point in writing a report.

4. Making an Outline: Once the final pattern of the report has taken shape in the writer's mind he should prepare an outline to write the report. In this outline, the problem is confirmed, the facts are recorded, they are analysed, and the rational conclusion is reached at. An outline is not essential, but it should be found extremely helpful in writing a systematic report.

5. Writing the Report: The last stage is report writing. It will require a continuous shuttling between the outline and the notes. First a rough outline of the report is made. Then it is revised, pruned, and refined. If the writer has more time at his hand, he will find it helpful to return to his rough outline after, say, a couple of days. This little gap will make his review work actually meaningful. The writer should also be careful about the langrage of the report. The report should be easy, clear, and free from grammatical mistakes. Finally, typing is done in an appropriate form and submits it.

3.6: Essentials of Good Report

Every business report should incorporate the following features.

1. Clarity: The business report should be entirely clear and completely understandable. This is possible if the author of the report has clear reason and thought in his mind. Not only clarity of thought, but also clarity of expression is essential.

2. Consistency: The business report should be consistent with the rationale of writing. The various stages in writing report like enquiry and collection of facts, their analysis and interpretation, and recommendations should flow towards the main theme.

3. User Oriented: Report is basically meant for the person who reads, not for the writer himself. If the words, symbols, and sentences used in report are beyond the reader's mental filter, the rationale of writing report will be defeated. Therefore, report should be modified according to user's communication ability.

4. Objectivity: There should be objectivity in observation, collection of related facts, and writing of report. Objectivity enhances the reliability and trustworthiness of the report. If biased, false and fabricated stories and findings are detected by the reader then the whole work will be in suspicion.

5. Accuracy: Accuracy of facts and figures is imperative for report. A misstatement of facts in statutory report results in heavy penalty under law. Incorrect and unfinished information in Non-statutory report misleads the management thereby resulting in taking wrong decisions and actions.

6. Brevity: The report should be made brief to save the reader's time and to retain his attention. Unnecessary details, irrelevant facts, and needless duplication of the same idea should be avoided.

7. Interesting: Business report should not only be informative and illuminating, but also be interesting to the person who reads it. If the reader's attention is not aroused and retained, he is likely to miss the parts of message. Report should look like living commentary, not dead and dull record.

8. Relevant: The report should be relevant for the user to make decisions. It will not be just post-mortem analysis for the sake of finding the causes.

9. Tone: The tone of the report is more formal than the tone for business letters or memos. It is customary to write the report in impersonal third person.

3.7: Summary

Report is a written or oral statement of truth connecting to a specific event. It is a significant document that assists in decision making. The main important objective of a report is to give information regarding any event to the appropriate authority. It is difficult to clearly define and demarcate the categories of business reports. Business reports may be classified on different basis like legal requirement, formality, frequency, functions, subject matter, writers, etc. Report can be organized in three ways. These are **Letter form, Memorandum form, and Letter text combination**

form. Five steps are suggested in preparing a report. These are investigating the source of information, taking notes, analysing the data, making an outline, and writing the report. Every business report should incorporate the features like clarity, consistency, user oriented, objectivity, accuracy, brevity, tone, relevant, and interesting.

3.8: Glossary

Analytical Report: An analytical report is not only contains the facts, views and opinions of reporters and others but also includes the causes for an issue or an event and required remedial action with recommendations.

Appendix: Statistical data, charts, and diagrams that are not generally included in the main body of the report are mentioned here.

Bibliography: This is a list of books and journals which are taken into consideration prior to or during the preparation of a report.

Formal Report: Formal reports are prepared as per the formal structure and established rules and presented before the appropriate authority.

Glossary: A glossary is a list of some technical or special words with their explanations.

Index: This is an alphabetical list of subjects of the report. An index assists the reader to trace any topic simply and quickly.

Informal Report: Informal report is prepared as per the ease of the reporter and presented before the person as per the requirement.

Informational Report: The Informational reports only present the facts and summary without analysing, interpreting, and making recommendations.

Non Statutory Report: Non-statutory reports are made not because of legal compulsion but because of necessity.

Routine Report: Routine report is made and presented to the director at particular intervals.

Specific Report: This report is made and presented to the top level management on specific request.

Statutory Report: Statutory reports are prepared in order to fulfil the legal compliance.

3.9: Self-Assessment Questions

1. Define report.
2. Discuss the objectives of preparing report.
3. Describe various kinds of reports.
4. Discuss the layout of a report.
5. What steps are to be followed in report writing?
6. What are the prerequisites of a good report?

Chapter-4

Business Language and Presentation

Contents

4.10: Self-Assessment Questions

4.0: Learning Objectives

After studying this unit, you will be capable to

- Understand the importance of business language;
- Appreciate vocabulary words often confused– discussed with examples;
- Comprehend words often miss spelt–discussed with the reference to 'Spelling Rules';
- Know common errors in English–discussed with examples;
- Know public speaking, meaning, pattern, essential steps of public speeches;
- Comprehend power point presentation-uses and advantages–discussed with an example of presentation slides;
- Know audio visual aids: types, uses, basic principles and guidelines for audio visual aids.

4.1: Importance of Business Language

The functional importance of business language for an individual or an organization cannot be overemphasized. Whether you are working as an executive in a multinational company, or an engineer working in a plant, or a scientist working in a premier scientific lab or a technical student in a professional institute, you need to explore business language. It is believed that business language will be in demand across occupations well into the next century. Effective business language is the foundation of any business organization. It helps to develop interpersonal understanding and enhances a person's ability to understand and solve the complicated problem in a business.

4.2: Vocabulary Words Often Confused

There are some words with the same pronunciation but different meaning. These are very confusing. A short list of such words is given below:

Sl. No	Words	Meaning	Applications
1	Accept Except	Take Leaving out	The manager has accepted the proposal given by his subordinate. He announced that every boy except his son have an access to the courts of law.
2	Accede Exceed	Agree Surpass	My friend accedes to my proposal. Write a paragraph on 'Global Worming' not exceeding 300 words.
3	Access Excess	Approach Additional	All the citizens of India should have access to the courts of law. Excess of power makes the politician arrogant.
4	Addition Edition	Putting more Form in which a book is published	Would you like to have card in addition to the other dishes? He bought a cheaper edition of a novel.
5	Affect Effect	To pretend To accomplish	I was too much affected to answer. The medicine has its side effect.
6	Adapt Adept Adopt	Accommodate to Skilful Take an idea, a custom, etc	Debadrita should adapt herself to the new situation. My daughter is adept in cooking. I like your methods of teaching and will adopt in my college.
7	Alter Altar	Change in character Raised candle for offering in temple or church	Debadrita's suit is too long and needs to be altered. After the examination, Abir lit ten candles at the altar.
8	Antic Antique	Odd, strange Old, ancient	The antics of the clown in the circus made us all laugh. My mother is very fond of collecting antique furniture.
9	Apposite Opposite	Proper, suitable Contrary	She made a number of arguments apposite to the case. His brother built a house opposite to the temple.
10	Assay Essay	Test of fineness or purity A part of composition	Mr. Roy called a meteorologist to make an assay of the ore. The essay has been written nicely.
11	Assent Ascent	Agree Going up	Debadrita give her assent to the proposal. The ascent to the peak of Everest is very difficult.
12	Berth Birth	A sleeping space in a train or bus Born	Please reserve for me a first Class AC birth in Satabdi Express. Dipanjana gave birth to a girl child
13	Bridal Bridle	of marriage part of the horse's harness	The mother- in -law expects a lot of bridal The horse trainer bridal the dangerous wild horse
14	Career Carrier	Profession / occupation Support system for a luggage/shipper	Dr. Dipsikha Chatterjee is very successful in her academic career The goods train is the biggest carrier of goods in India.

15	Censer Censor	A pot in which incense is burnt An official board to permit the publication of boos or films	Put the incense in the censor The film censor board has a contribution to Indian films.
16	Cite Site Sight	Quote Place where something was or is to be View or scene	Mrs. Dipannita cited many examples to her juniors Dr. Debadrita is looking for a suitable site to establish a college I have lost my sight.
17	Curtsy Courtesy	Posture to show respect Polite manners	The employees of star category hotels were taught to make curtsy to the hotel guest This program is presented by courtesy of Tata and Reliance Group
18	Desert Dessert	Land without water and full of sand Sweet dish served after lunch or dinner	Name the biggest desert in the world We used to take ice cream as dessert after having lunch
19	Gild Guild	To have a thin covering of gold Association of a professionals	The bride refused to wear gilded jewellery The middle aged members of a guild helped each other for furthering their common interest
20	Jealous Zealous	Envious enthusiastic	He was jealous of his friend's increasing popularity The newly joined employee is zealous to satisfy his employer
21	Raise Raze	To lift up To destroy	Sheela raised many objections in the Board Meeting The huts were razed to the ground

4.3: Words Often Miss Spelt

Very often we spell words by sheer force of habit. Sometimes, when in doubt, by writing the concerned words we can recollect their correct spelling. There are a number of rules for spelling words. A few are given below:

4.4: Common Errors in English

A common errors often made in the use of articles, nouns, pronouns, adjectives, verbs, infinitives gerunds, and prepositions. A few examples of each segment are given below for reference.

Sl. No:	Rules	Implications
1	The silent e occurring at the end is dropped in words when a suffix beginning with ***a vowel*** is added to them	Behave Behaviour Admire Admirable Arrive Arriving
2	The silent e is retained in words ending in ce and ge when a suffix other than that beginning with ***e or i*** is added to them	Service Serviceable Charge Charging Courage Courageous
3	In a monosyllabic word, ending in a consonant and preceded by a single vowel letter, *the consonant is doubled if a suffix beginning with a vowel letter is added to it*	Big Bigger Win Winner Hot Hottest
4	If a word ends in *two consonants or one consonant* *Preceded by two vowel letters* the *consonant does not double before any suffix*	Feed Feeding Wait Waiter Wood Wooden
5	In a multisyllabic word ending in *one vowel letter l* *the l is doubled if a suffix beginning with a vowel is added to it*	Travel Traveller Repel Repellant Pedal Pedalled
6	If the final y of a word is preceded by a consonant the y *changes to i before all suffixes except ing*	Study Studies Dry Dries Supply Supplies

1. Use of Articles

Incorrect	Correct
The sinner was condemned to the hell.	The sinner was condemned to hell.
Dr. Debadrita is MP.	Dr. Debadrita is an MP.
It is written in Gita that God incarnates.	It is written in the Gita that God incarnates.
It is the moral duty of a man to help a poor.	It is the moral duty of a man to help the poor.
Honesty is a best policy.	Honesty is the best policy.

1. Use of Noun

Incorrect	Correct
Switzerland is very famous for beautiful sceneries.	Switzerland is very famous for beautif scenery.
I have a ten rupees note which is torn.	I have a ten rupee note which is torn.
Munnabhai as failed in this, but he will appear in the next examination.	Munn bhai as failed in this examination, bu he will appear in the next.
Debu's,the grocer's business is flourishing	Debu, the grocer's business is flourishing
She has six brother –in –laws	She has six brothers –in –laws

1. Use of Pronouns

Incorrect	Correct
He has resigned to his fate.	He has resigned himself to his fate.
It is I who is to blame.	It is I who am to blame.
Many persons who we know, are hypocrites.	Many persons whom we know, are hypocrites
Man cannot get all what he wants.	Man cannot get all that he wants.
Let you and I solve the problem.	Let you and me solve the problem.

1. Use of Adjectives

Incorrect	Correct
She is superior than me.	She is superior to me.
We often find the kind of things.	We often find things of this kind.
She has the best voice of any singer.	She has a better voice than any other singer.
She is elder than me.	She is older than me.
He is a most perfect gentleman.	He is a perfect gentleman.

1. Use of Verbs

Incorrect	Correct
The army do not present a smart appearance.	The army does not present a smart·appearanc
Every men and women were killed in the battle.	Every men and women was killed in the battl
The committee is divided in their opinion about nuclear policy.	The committee are divided in their opinion ab nuclear policy.
Dr. Debamita has returned from USA yesterday.	Dr. Debamita returned from USA yesterday.
Keep this on the table.	Put this on the table.

1. Use of Infinitives, Gerunds

Incorrect	Correct
You should aim to please other.	You should aim at pleasing other.
Mr. Roy intended to have gone there.	Mr. Roy intended to go there.
She can avail of this.	She can avail herself of this.
Please forgive me being rude.	Please forgive me for being rude.
It is nothing else than vanity.	It is nothing else but vanity.

1. Use of Prepositions

Incorrect	Correct
He is enamored of the new actress.	He is enamored with the new actress.
His mother cannot approve her conduct.	His mother cannot approve of her conduct.
Christmas corresponds with Deepabali.	Christmas corresponds to Deepabali.
Send the parcel on this address.	Send the parcel to this address.
Sumit prevailed on all difficulties.	Sumit prevailed over all difficulties.

4.5: Public Speaking

It is said that 'Speech' is a gift of nature. In fact it can instil new zeal, uplift sagging confidence and soothe injured feelings. Hitler once remarked "All epoch making revolutionary events have been produced not by the written word but by the spoken word".

Generally Public speaking means speaking to a group of persons or audience on a subject that is professional in nature. Some speaking situation one has to speak publicly at the workplace is as follows:

- Lecture on a specific subject
- Briefing employees on a certain issue
- Addressing a general body meeting
- Paper presentation in a seminar
- Inaugurating an official event

In this context, the first thing that we need to understand that 'public speaking' is not an inborn talent; it is a set of skills that is acquired by constant efforts. Let us discuss some of the essential features of public speaking and learn ways to make the task interesting, purposeful, and rewarding.

4.5.1: Pattern

As a speaker, the first thing that one has to do is to structure one's speech. Before speeches are delivered formally, the speaker has to decide the pattern in which the idea will be put across to the audience. There are some recognized patterns which you can choose any one of these or use some of these.

1.Chronological Pattern: Chronological pattern is used to organize a speech. In this pattern, we arrange ideas, keeping in mind the chronology of events. For example, if we want to give a speech on 'The Development of Psychology', 'The Progress of Democracy in the World', 'The History of Indian cricket', etc., we have to choose a series of events and speak about their development over a period of time. To use this pattern, it is needed to match the sequence of events and time. The speeches organized through this pattern require a clear link to be established between the events and time sequence.

2.Casual Pattern: In this pattern the ideas are divided into two major components-causes and their effects. Normally this pattern is been chosen to highlight the relationship between a problem and the reason behind it. The examples of some of the topics which require the structure the speech in this pattern are 'Global Warming', 'Impact of Advertisements on Young Generations', 'Smoking: Its Causes and Effects, etc. The casual pattern is chosen in situations when the speaker intends to create a lasting impact on his /her listeners.

3.Topical Pattern: Another commonly used pattern is the topical pattern where different parts of speech have to divide and arrange and plot them into various heading and sub headings. When the speaker has to address his/her audience about a specific topic with various kinds / types it is recommended to use this pattern. Some of the topics for which you may select the topical pattern for arranging the ideas of your speech are 'Importance of Sex Education in Schools', 'Kinds of Cyclonic storms', etc.

4.Spatial Pattern: Spatial pattern is the best suited to speeches which have a geographical or structural orientation. This pattern is widely used to arrange the discussion in different directions, it is also known as 'Directional Pattern'. For instance, topics such as 'Mysore Palace: Its structure and splendour', 'Design of an Automated Washing Machine', 'The Birla Temple, Jaipur: A structural Description', etc. would fall under this category.

5.Psychological Pattern: The speeches structured in the Psychological Pattern are quite emotive in style and sense. In these situations, the speaker arranges ideas in a manner most likely to create an immediate impact on the listeners. Here is some topics speaking on which the speakers may use this pattern are: 'Nuclear Family', Loneliness, etc.

4.5.2: Essential Steps of Public Speaking

We would like to discuss some major steps which can improve the ability for public speaking.

1. Preparatory Steps: Preparations is essential for a successful public speaking. It is said "The best preparation for tomorrow is doing your best today". If you take the following steps, you would normally be well prepared for the event.

a) Gather the Relevant Information: The first step you should gather the relevant information from different sources like newspapers, journals, books, internet, website, etc., and note it down in an organized way in Note Cards. Most speakers prefer to prepare an outline of speech and the main points, sub points and key words. These are helpful for a speaker to recall the particular matter to be presented. Other preparatory steps to which attention is to pay is the inspection of venue of speech which include: the sitting arrangements of the venue, position of the podium, screen to display the matter, technical support, etc. This information would put you in proper frame of mind and help you to perform better.

b) Structuring the Contents: It is customary to divide the contents into three parts namely: Introduction, Main Body, and Conclusion.

Introduction part has to handle by the speaker very carefully as it has a great impact on the audience. In a way, at the initial stage, speaking in public is like riding a horse. Once you manage to settle firmly in the saddle, it would go galloping to the goal. In this stage, the speaker needs to establish a rapport with the audience. There are some ways to motivate the audience to listen to you. Given below a few elements that can be included in the introduction:

a) Narrate the objective of the speech clearly

b) Give a preview of what you are going to say

c) Relate the topic to the need or interest of the audience

d) Establish your credibility

e) Grow the curiosity among the audience

f) Make a dramatic statement

g) Give complements to the audience.

Main Body: In this stage, the key ideas are presented. The presentation of the idea together with explanatory and supporting documents takes about ninety percent of the total allotted time. So, it is necessary to make extra efforts to handle the contents of the main body.

Given below a few elements that should be included in the Main body of your presentation:

i) Presentation pattern has to be identified very carefully. The most commonly used pattern is the arrangement of sub-topics and modules constituting them into an order of their relative importance.

ii) Developing of points is very important to maintain the sequence and presented the matter successfully. A few common devices used for this purpose. Examples like Comparison and Contrast, Statistics, Testimony, Definition, etc.

- **Conclusion:** If you have successfully covered up the Introduction and Main Body, the audience would expect you to end it with an interesting and powerful punch. According to the noted author H.W. Longfellow, 'Great is the art of beginning but greater is the art of ending'. The attention level of the audience is likely to be high at this stage. Like preparing the earlier parts, there is a need to map out clearly how you would conclude your speech. It is suggested not to leave it for further decision till the moment comes. If you keep in focus the function of the conclusion, it would be not at all difficult to end your speech effectively. Usually a good conclusion repeats concisely the central idea.

4.6: Power Point Presentation

All most all personal computers come with different software packages already installed in them. One of the most widely used packages is Power Point. Power point presentation enables to create a document called presentation which is used for communicating ideas, thoughts, and messages to the audience.

4.6.1: Uses of Power Point Presentation

Power point presentation is mainly used in business, projects, and academic arena for different purposes such as marketing projects, business strategies, research work, etc. Power point presentation helps us to structure information efficiently. It offers charts, graphs, and animation effects to maximize the impact of the presentation. Besides, it provides ready- to- use sample presentation for consultations.

On the basis of Microsoft Power Point, one can use a feature called 'Auto Content Wizard' a tool that would guide you through the process of customizing a predesigned document. Presentation Graphics Software provides formats with complementary colours for background. You can also make use of Presentation Dialog Box that enables you to choose essential features of a basic presentation.

Let us take an example of the presentation slides of a presentation of a research paper on Women's Literacy in India' may have the following slides:·

Title: Women's Literacy in India
Presenter: Dr. Adrita

Slide 1

Census years	Male (%)	Introduction Literacy Rate Femal (%)
1951	26.16	08.86
1961	40.40	15.35
1971	45.96	21.97
1981	56.38	29.76
1991	64.13	39.29
2001	75.85	54.16
2011	78.12	56.38

Slide 2

Factors Responsible

- Gender based inequality
- Social Discrimination
- Role Definition
- Engage of Girl Child in Domestic Work
- Low Enrolment of Girl Child in Schools

Slide 3

Measures Taken by the Society and Government

- Initiative Taken by the Society
- Initiative From Government

Slide 4

Benefits of Female Literary

- Women's Empowerment
- Better living Status of Women
- Economic Independency
- Women Entrepreneur
- Better Education and Health
- Gender Equality
- Development of Women

Slide 5 | **Conclusion**

4.6.2: Advantages of Power Point Presentation

The main advantage of Power Point Presentation is to view the slides, change the contents, edit the matter, and make different backgrounds for different slides. One can take off a few slides and add new ones in their place. The matter given in the slides should also be in the form of 'Note Cards'.

4.7: Audio Visual Aids

A professional has to make an oral presentation in various programs. The use of audio visual aids makes the presentation smooth. The term 'Audio Visual Aids' refers to the equipment available to us for amplifying our message. An aid thus makes the communication vivid, stimulating, and interesting. An aid is not merely a help to the audience but also to the speaker.

In specific terms, we are concerned with the following audio-visual aids: white board/Black board, overhead projector, filmstrip and slide projector, movie film projector, VCD and DVD players.

4.7.1: Types of Audio Visual Aids and Their Use

a) White Board/Black Board

This is the most easily available visual aid equipment. It is very cost effective aid and requiring minimum expertise. Some of the advantages in the use of these boards are mentioned below:

- A board offers plenty of space to the user to write and present drawings, diagrams, maps, graphs.
- It gives the audience a feeling of spontaneity.
- The board permits the progressive development of a design, process or idea which will sustain the interest of the audience.

b) Overhead Projector

It is a popular audio visual tool which is versatile in nature and relatively inexpensive aid to the speaker. The projector is placed on a table approximately 9 ft. away from the screen. Display material is put on transparencies. You can simply write or draw on a transparency or you may photocopy on a transparency the printed material you wish to display. You may prepare the transparencies beforehand or you may build up the information you wish to project in the time of presentation.

c) Filmstrip and Slide Projector

Filmstrips are a sequence of transparencies on 8 or 16 mm films. They are commercially produced but can be prepared by professionals to meet the special need. It can be handled easily. The sequence of projection cannot be changed.

d) Movie Film Projector

This medium is now being used not only for entertainment but also for teaching, training, and advertising. Films are available in four sizes- 8 mm,16 mm, 35 mm and 70 mm with sound. For teaching and training purpose 16 mm format are generally used.

Before showing a film prepare your audience by a short introduction and after the show is over, conduct a meaningful discussion, ending the session with a summary. It is essential that the film is of sufficient merit to justify its inclusion in your plan. It must be previewed so that it can be properly integrated with your presentation.

e) VCD and DVD Players

The use of video equipment is now becoming commonplace. Any display material requiring visual motion and sound can be recorded or downloaded on a compact disc (CD) and used for presentation on VCD or DVD players. It is easy to handle a player and to monitor a television set. The equipment is easily portable. Thus, for teaching a small audience this medium can be chosen as an aid in the presentation.

4.7.2: Basic Principles and Guidelines for Audio –Visual Aids

The following are the basic guidelines to use an Audio -Video Aids:

i) Contents to finalize for which the Audio Visual Aid will be used

ii) Choose the appropriate medium

iii) Incorporate the aid with the presentation

iv) A basic knowledge to gather to use operate the equipment

v) Inspect the venue of presentation, if possible, to check the physical arrangements such as switches, power supply, size of the venue, pointer, etc.

vi) Preparation of audio visual material with utmost care

vii) When you use several items of visual material, number them. Ensure that their appearance and exit are properly timed.

4.8: Summary

In the first phase of this chapter we have focused on the importance of business language for an individual or an organization. There is a need to explore business language for any profession or business organization. It is believed that business language will be in demand across occupations and is identified as valuable for both employment and job performance. Effective business language is the foundation of any business organization.

We have identified that there are some words with the same pronunciation but different meaning which are very confusing. A short list of such words has been given with examples.

In the next part, we have focused on the words with correct spelling and mentioned a number of rules for spelling words in reference to the Spelling Rules. Also we have observed that the common errors often made in the use of articles, nouns, pronouns, adjectives, verbs, infinitives gerunds, and prepositions. A few examples of each segment are given for reference.

In the next phase, we have discussed the importance of public speaking for a professional career. There are five patterns for organizing your ideas: Chronological Pattern, Casual Pattern, Topical Pattern, Spatial Pattern, and Psychological Pattern. You can choose any of these patters or blend of these as per your requirement.

We have discussed some of the major steps which can improve the ability for public speaking which included firstly the preparatory steps where gather the relevant information is very important. Secondly, it is important to structure the contents. A few common devices used for this purpose like Comparison and Contrast, Statistics, Testimony, Definition, etc. In conclusion part, there is a need to map out clearly how you would conclude your speech. It is suggested not to leave it for further decision till the moment comes. If you keep in focus the function of the conclusion, it would be not at all difficult to end your speech effectively. Usually a good conclusion repeats concisely the central idea.

Next, we have stated the Power Point Presentation and its uses. For reference we have put an example of the presentation slides.

Next, we have discussed on the Audio Visual Aids - different types of Audio Visual Aids like White Board/Black Board, Overhead Projector, Filmstrip and Slide Projector, Movie Film Projector, VCD and DVD Players with reference to their applications. Basic principles and guidelines for Audio –Visual Aids such as contents, choosing the appropriate medium, time management, incorporating the aid with the presentation have been discussed.

4.9: Glossary

Audio Visual Aids: It refers to the equipment available to us for amplifying our message.

Auto Content Wizard: It is a tool that would guide you through the process of customizing a predesigned document.

Casual Pattern: In this pattern, the ideas are divided into two major components-causes and their effects.

Chronological Pattern: Chronological pattern is the commonly used pattern for organizing a speech.

Dialog Box: It enables you to choose essential features of a basic presentation.

Filmstrip and Slide Projector: Filmstrips are a sequence of transparencies on 8 or 16 mm films.

Movie Film Projector: This medium is now being used not only for entertainment but also for teaching, training, and advertising.

Overhead Projector: It is a popular audio visual tool which is versatile in nature and relatively inexpensive aid to the speaker.

Power Point Presentation: It is one of the most widely used packages is Power Point. Power point presentation enables to create a document called presentation which is used for communicating ideas, thoughts, and messages to the audience.

Psychological Pattern: The speeches structured in the psychological pattern are quite emotive in style and sense.

Public Speaking: Public speaking means speaking to a group of persons or audience on a subject that is professional in nature.

Topical Pattern: It is a commonly used pattern is the topical pattern where different parts of speech have to divide and arrange and plot them into various heading and sub headings.

VCD and DVD Players: Any display material requiring visual motion and sound can be recorded or downloaded on a compact disc (CD) and used for presentation on VCD or DVD players.

4.10: Self-Assessment Questions

1. State the importance ofBusiness Language in professional career.

2. State why Spelling is important in Business Language with reference to the Spelling Rules:

3. Why public speaking is necessary to build a professional career?

4. 'In delivering a speech patterns of organization and modes of delivery play a significant role'. Highlight the importance and suitability of each of these patterns generally employed in the speech making process.

5. Discuss the essential steps of Public Speaking.

6. What is 'Power Point Presentation'? What are the uses of Power Point Presentation? What is the advantage of using Power Point Presentation?

7. Prepare a power point presentation on "Global Worming: Causes and effect".

8. What do you mean by 'Audio Visual Aids'? State the various types of Audio Visual Aids and their uses.

9. Discuss the basic principles and guidelines for Audio – Visual Aids.

Chapter-5

Technology and Business Communication

Contents

5.0: Learning Objectives

After studying this unit, you will be capable to

- Understand the role, effects, and advantages of technology in business communication;
- Know about various technologies used in business communication;
- Comprehend the modern techniques in business communication;
- Visualize the strategic importance of e-communication.

5.1: Role of Technology in Business Communication

Nowadays, we cannot think any business which can run without technology. Any business that has disregarded technology either has been kicked out of the market or is not making profits. Technology is now becoming the strategic tool of communication. It is time to understand the role of technology in business communication. Technology carries business communication role. Without it, business communication would return to the early dark ages where it took days or weeks for information to be passed. That is why any business should not overlook the technological role. Technology drives change and communication is one of the roles that cannot be done better without technology. Various roles of technology in business communication are stated below:

i) Specific Targeting of Communication Recipients

It is not everybody who should be receiving all the communication from a business. That is why technology has brought about targeting a specific group with a set of information. If a business chooses to communicate to the teens, the most excellent way to reach them is through social media. For the adult age group, a business would use television and newspapers. In a nutshell, technology has made it feasible for business communication to be targeted to a specific group.

ii) It Makes Communication More Effective

With technology, a business can decide how to communicate to a certain group of customers. It could use telephony, social media, blogs or email. A business can pass its information more effectively.

iii) Prompt Communication

Without technology, business communication was hectic. It could take days for information to be created and dispersed. Today, it only takes pressing a button, and all is done. Business can now communicate instantly thus addressing its customers not only effectively but also in a fast manner.

iv) Diversification of Business Communication

There are various communication methods at the disposal of any business. It comes down to the kind of communication and the target audience. There are emails, mobile devices, websites, blogs, newsletters and so much more. Business communication is now more diversified and thus can reach any place and anybody on the planet. This is the power that every business should apply to communicate successfully to its customers.

v) Minimizing the Cost of Business Communication

Without technology, it was not cheap to create and pass information. Today, some businesses do not even need a budget for communication. Some only use an insignificant amount towards their communication role. Technology has cut down all the barriers that would require a hefty budget for communication to be effective and efficient. You cannot imagine how cumbersome and costly communication would be without technology.

vi) Collaboration of Information

Today, thanks to technology, businesses can apply them the same piece of information on different platforms. Information created on a computer may be used on a website, send an email, posted on social platforms or shared via blogs. This collaboration of information has helped business cut down the workforce needed in the communication process. That not only makes business communication better but also simplifies the task regarding expenses.

5.2: Effects of Technology in Business Communication

Technology has changed our lifestyle and it will be continuing. Actually, there is **no aspect** in our life that technology has not reached. However, technology has made a profound impact on communication.

Technology has made an enormous positive impact on communication but it cannot be denied that there is also a negative side. First, let's take a look at technology's **negative impact on communication:**

i) Quality Suffers

With the help of technology we are doing multitasking. We are now able to perform many functions simultaneously in a short duration of time. Consequently, our focus is really in fragments. We cannot make any meaningful connection. Therefore, quality of communication suffers.

ii) Virtual Rather than Personal

The easy availability of various communication devices makes the communication virtual rather than personal touch. You may make a video call to anyone but on that time you are giving more attention to our phone rather than with the person to whom you are talking.

There are also positive **effects of technology in business communication:**

i) Fast and Easy

Communication has now become very fast due to the advent of sophisticated technological devices. We may connect anyone within a second. Business can now easily connect to their clients. Therefore, any problem can be settled very fast. We are now enjoying the speed of communication in every sphere of business.

ii) Easy Access

Now, we have various communication devices through which we can easily access to any one in the globe. We can now perform various business related activities from our home also. Technology enables us to make work life balance.

iii) More Productive

We have become more productive due to technology concerning to business communication. We can now perform any business activities very fast. Business communication has now become very easy due to the availability of different user friendly technologies at our disposal. We get maximum output by employing very less input in terms of time and cost.

5.3: Advantages of Technology in Business Communication

Technology has made the workplace more efficient and has increased productivity. It's easy to keep updated information, file your work and share with others. As technology continues to impact the work procedure, it's important for us to stay constantly learning and opened to new initiatives that could positively impact our daily lives.

Significant businesses around the world are conscious that technology has drastically changed the method we perform today. At the inception of digital era, we took some time to adapt the digital age but the reward was invaluable. The most important benefits of technology applied in business communications are stated below:

i) Increased Communication: Do you remember a time at work when you had to dispatch a handwritten letter to your boss who might have worked in a different location due to either travel meetings or important projects? The normal reply time might have been days. At present, technology provides us the ample chance to communicate via email, messages, etc. within a second from every corner of the globe.

ii) Improved Security and Distribution: in the past, we used to keep heaps of paperwork in a locked safe cabinet or locker. Nowadays, technology permits businesses to keep thousands of valuable information and important files on a single Personal Computer, external hard disc or in a cloud drive. We are now also using various ant viruses in order to protect our devices from hacking. The appropriate authorities have only access to these files and can share among themselves within seconds and keep the files safe and secured.

iii) Visual Quality: Do you memorize those days when you used to write reports using typewriter? During that time, you had to perform it cautiously to maintain proper quality? Currently, computers have various software tools like MS Word, Excel, and PowerPoint, etc. which can compose your reports more visually beautiful. We can also detect mistakes in words or grammatical mistakes in sentences.

iv) Quick and Accessible Information: The Internet is another innovation in technology which is applied in business communication. Trips to this virtual library can take place within seconds. Getting the material you are looking for has never been easier and/or faster. Have you heard of a single company that doesn't use internet in their daily basis? That's right, today having Internet access is as important as having a computer, because of the accessible information you can receive while using it at work, which can increase knowledge and substance different work reports.

v) Increased Efficiency: Last but not the least is efficiency. At present, most of the functions are performed through the machine. In the manufacturing industry, almost all the manual functions have been replaced by the automated machines. Consequently, production cost has been reduced remarkably. In the case of service industry, all the services are now rendered to the clients with the help of advanced and sophisticated devices. Consequently, we have increased the efficiency manifolds.

5.4: Various Technologies in Business Communication

5.4.1: Email

Email is the most popular business communication device in recent years. We can get maximum advantages by using email. Using email, we can communicate with workers and customers, schedule meetings, send automatic notifications and share newsletters with old as well as new customers. Email has also been used by some scammers and hackers in recent years, so it is important to be vigilant for fraudulent messages.

Email has now become the significant method of business communication that is very fast, inexpensive, easily accessible, and duplicated. Businesses get immense benefits by using email as a means of business communication as it provides efficient as well as effective ways to transfer all types of electronic data.

Advantages of Using Email

We can get the following advantages of using email in business communication:

Cheap: The cost of sending email is very low and the cost remains same at any distance and the cost is not dependent on the number of recipients.

Fast: We can send our information at a very high speed to the recipients using email.

Convenient: It is very easy to handle. Our message will be automatically stored until the receivers receive it. We can also send the same information to other people.

Permanent: We can also keep detailed records of all sending or receiving information into the mail box.

One of the key **advantages of email** is that you can speedily and easily send all types of electronic files like as text documents, photographs and excel data sheets to numerous contacts by attaching the respective file to an email. We can also extend the size of,attachments on a special request to the internet service provider as per the need of the business. There are also some options that we can set to our email software for making automatic entries in our address book for every sending or receiving message. There is also automatic reply option to ensure the receipt of an order or anyone can easily get the information about you whether you are not into the office or you are on leave.

Disadvantages of Using Email

Despite the numerous benefits, there are some flaws of using email which are stated below:

Spam: Sometimes, unwanted email may devastate your email system unless you install a firewall and anti-spam software. There may be raised internet and email security issues, particularly if you work using the cloud or remote access.

Viruses: It may easily penetrate into the attachments through email.

Sending Emails by Mistake: An email may reach to the wrong recipient by your wrong click of a button and may disclose the confidential as well as sensitive information of your business to other recipients. You must take care of it when you are sending any mail to the recipients. You can minimize the incidents of data theft or leakage if you give proper attention at the time of sending your data files.

Data Storage: There is also the space problem to store the data when large attachments are sent or received through email.

5.4.2: Text Messaging

Short Message Service (SMS) or text messages have a place in the digital business communication toolbox. One useful feature of an SMS network is the capacity to broadcast short bursts of information to mobile devices in the case of an emergency. There are other applications which fall into the "do not reply" category, such as one-way text messaging services that are widely used. Now, we get various mobile messages concerning to the due date of electricity bills, due date of insurance premium, debit or credit information of our bank accounts, etc. Nowadays, companies are also taking advantage of SMS technology for various marketing campaigns to connect customers with automated prompts and responses.

SMS messaging service was first introduced in 1992 and has now become one of the most extensively used attributes on any type of mobile phone. According to the study conducted by the Pew Research Centre based in Washington DC, SMS messaging is the most commonly used smart phone feature. Young smart phone users are also very mush prone to text messaging services.

We have given here some examples when SMS messaging is the better option for business communications:

i) SMS is a widespread communication device and can be sent to any mobile phone.

ii) SMS can be sent to rural areas or areas having poor internet connectivity.

iii) SMS provides reliable communications.

iv) SMS offers brief and comprehensible communications with various stakeholders of business.

5.4.3: Instant Messaging

Instant messaging is one kind of online conversation that allows you to send and receive concise written messages in real time. A lot of organizations apply instant messaging for one-on-one conversations and group conversation. A few popular instant messaging apps include Google Hangouts, Slack, and HipChat.

Instant messaging is defined as a type of exchanging text messages in real time. These messages can be received or sent by an individual or a group of individuals by using a private or public instant messaging network. Here, both the sender and the receiver must apply the similar network to share the messages. You can take the advantage of instant messaging system from any electronic devise like smart phone, laptop or desktop, tablet, etc.

Advantages of Instant Messaging for Business Communication

Cost Effective Communication

Instant messaging services permit you to communicate with anyone located in any part of the globe without any call tariffs. The businesses can easily communicate with the overseas suppliers by sending them instant messages. Therefore, it makes the communication cost effective.

Real-Time Communication

Real time communication is possible using instant messaging system. It is faster than emails. In case of email, you have to wait for response until your messages is retrieved from the server by the recipients. Using instant messaging system, business can get quick response from the customers end. It can also be very much useful for internal communication purpose.

Building a Team

Instant messaging system helps to communicate freely among the team members in real time without any interruption. In telephonic communication, information may be distorted or misunderstood. In that case, instant messaging system can be very much effective tool for communication among the team members. This system is very much fruitful when the team members are geographically separated from each other or they are located at long distances.

Convenience

Instant messaging system is very much convenient rather than the telephonic communication. In the telephonic communication, you have to give proper attention to make the communication effective. Under the telephonic conversation, you have to only concentrate on a phone call leaving all other works. Under Instant messaging system, you may also perform other tasks simultaneously.

Reduction of Spam Messages

Your inbox can be overloaded with a number of spam messages when you are using email. In instant messaging system such type of situation will not be raised anytime.

Archiving

Record keeping option is also available into the instant messaging software. Your all messages will be saved as archives which you can use as reference whenever you like to do that.

Disadvantages of Instant Messaging for Business Communication

Low Security

Instant messaging is not very much secured in comparison to other modes of communication. Instant messaging works on public network. Therefore, anyone could enter into the chat and could also observe the communication.

Workplace Distraction

Some businesses are worried about instant messaging system as all the employees engage themselves in most of the time which distract them from their actual work leads to lower productivity. There is a possibility if somebody wishes to chat while you have been already occupied with an important assignment.

5.5: Modern Techniques in Business Communication

5.5.1: Video Conferencing

It is a visual conference between two or more individuals in spite of their location, featuring audio and video content communication in real time.

For successful conferencing, business organizations require to set up a conferencing software and hardware solutions for rooms, personal computers, mobile devices, and browsers. Video conferencing consists of an endpoint (ranging from a PC to a telepresence system), video conferencing server, peripherals (webcam, microphone, headset, etc.) and software infrastructure (video processing, content transmission, integrations, etc.). it is a modern high-tech communication means for escalating efficiency for businesses, optimizing and accelerating decision-making processes, and reducing customer's and employee's travelling costs.

Video Conferencing Benefits

i) Save Your Time: You can save your valuable time through the video conferencing technique. You do not require any business vacation as you can connect easily connect with your colleagues from your PC or meeting room.

ii) Easy-to-Use: For video conferencing, you have to schedule your meeting with your colleagues and start video conferencing. Your conferencing software will remind you about the meeting time. It is very user friendly system and no additional training is required for video conferencing.

iii) Collaboration Tools: For effective workflow, this system provides diverse collaboration tools like as content and screen sharing, instant messaging, slideshow, etc. Under this system, many users can work jointly on a common project and they can easily share their various ideas as well as results.

iv) Real-life Impressions: Through video conferencing, visual contact is possible among the users. One can easily observe the others emotional expression during video conferencing. Video conferencing is very closer to real life situations. Moreover, it does not allow users to divert from each other as they give full concentration at the time of video conferencing.

v) Security: This system is based on particular codes, proprietary protocols, and actively using encryption to make the system fully secured.

5.5.2: Social Networking

Facebook Messenger: It is very popular around the world except China and Iran. It is one of the top three most admired social networking sites of almost each country. It has very large markets in United States, Australia, Canada, etc.

WhatsApp: It is very popular messaging app around the world. Some remarkable exceptions include Denmark, Greece, Hungary, Norway, Poland, Romania, Argentina, Czech Republic, and Sweden where Facebook Messenger is more popular.

WeChat: It is a messaging app where you can only consider region and ethnicity. WeChat is very popular app in China. Chinese expatriates also use this app when they are in abroad. If you desire to connect with Chinese consumers then WeChat is the only messaging option before you as all other messaging apps are not used in China.

Blogs: It is place where you can write your opinion or you can discuss any particular topic of your interest. You may create your blog and communicate your opinions or information to others.

Facebook: The largest social network is now face book. You have to create your own account in face book in order to communicate various information or personal message to your face book friends. You can send a friend request to other face book users of your choice. Different companies may also create a face book page of their respective brands to make their brands very much popular in the market.

Twitter: It is also one kind of social network through which an individual or a group of individuals may express their opinions or status with a short message. The character limit of short message is 140.

YouTube & Video: Using this platform, you may upload any video in order to communicate any important information to the users. You can get various information through watching YouTube.

Flicker: It is an image and video hosting platform for online community. Photos can be shared in this platform.

Instagram: It is a platform through which photograph and video may be shared freely in different social networking sites. You can also give special effects to your photographs and videos through this platform.

Snapchat: It is a mobile messaging application. It is used to share photos, videos, text, and drawings. You can freely download this app and you can share your photos, videos, text, and drawings using this app. It has now become very popular app among the young generation. The unique feature of this app is that the snapchat message disappears from the recipient's mobile phone after a few seconds.

LinkedIn Groups: Through this LinkedIn groups, group of professionals can share various information among themselves.

Pinterest: It is one type of social network that permits users to share and find out new interests by posting images or videos to their own or others' boards and browsing what other users have pinned. The social network's objective is to "connect everybody in the globe through the 'things' they discover interesting." Users can either upload images from their computer or pin things they find on the web using the Pinterest book market.

TikTok: Today, TikTok is the world's number one platform. Through this platform, we can create a short video and post the video of up to 15 seconds. The upper limit for recording is 15 seconds. However, it can be extended up to 60 seconds long. Business can use this platform to display their newly launched products.

5.6: Strategic Importance of E-communication

E- Communication plays a significant role in contemporary business as well as society. We cannot imagine of passing modern life and managing contemporary businesses without electronic communication. It permits the amalgamation of numerous media, such as data, graphics, video, and sound, into one message. Devices such as cell phones with mobile communication technology and portable laptops enable people to stay in touch with friends and co-workers at all times.

Some issues are mentioned below in order to highlight the significance of this type of communication:

Quick Transmission of Information

The most advantage of electronic communication is the fast communication of information. With the assist of electronic media, anyone can send information to a remote receiver immediately. It takes a few seconds to communicate through electronic media as it helps quick transmission.

Communicating a Large Volume of Information

You can now send a huge quantity of information with the aid of electronic devices. Through e-mail, you can append writings of hundred pages without any difficulty. Due to the development of electronic media, business managers now can smoothly manage operation transversely around the world.

Wide Coverage

Through this e-communication, you can pass on information to numerous receivers who are situated in diverse places. With the aid of electronic devices like satellite, people have conquered distance and the entire world has now turned into a global village and communication around the globe needs a second only.

Lowering Communication Cost

Electronic communication not only saves time but also money. This communication such as e-mail requires less cost than the traditional means of posting a letter. Electronic communication saves time and money. For example, Text SMS is cheaper than the usual letter.

Making an Instant Business Decision

With the aid of electronic communication, business managers can take immediate decisions. With a single click of the computer, they can obtain information at any time from anyplace in the globe. This assists in taking an immediate decision and ensures better management of the business.

Easy Preservation of Information

Electronic devices can store up a vast quantity of information that can be used as and when required. Electronic communication permits the instant exchange of feedback. Consequently, communication becomes very much comfortable using electronic media. The use of manual files is diminishing day by day due to the e-communication.

Communication with Distant People

Electronic communication gives the opportunity for interactive communication with distant people. For example, video conferencing permits interactive communication although the participants are geographically isolated. It saves travel cost, time, and energy.

5.7: Summary

Technology is now becoming the strategic tool of communication. It is time to understand the role of technology in business communication. Technology carries business communication role. Without it, business communication would return to the early dark ages where it took days or weeks for information to be passed.

Technology has changed our lifestyle and it will be continuing. Technology has made the workplace more efficient and has increased productivity. It's easy to keep updated information, file your work and share with others. As technology continues to impact the work procedure, it's important for us to stay constantly learning and opened to new initiatives that could positively impact our daily lives.

5.8: Glossary

Blogs: It is place where you can write your opinion or you can discuss any particular topic of your interest.

Flicker: It is an image and video hosting platform for online community. Photos can be shared in this platform.

Instagram: It is a platform through which photograph and video may be shared freely in different social networking sites.

You can also give special effects to your photographs and videos through this platform.

Instant Messaging: Instant messaging is one kind of online conversation that allows you to send and receive concise written messages in real time.

Linked In Groups: Through this Linked In groups, group of professionals can share various information among themselves.

Pinterest: It is one type of social network that permits users to share and find out new interests by posting images or videos to their own or others' boards and browsing what other users have pinned.

Twitter: It is also one kind of social network through which an individual or a group of individuals may express their opinions or status with a short message. The character limit of short message is 140.

Video Conferencing: It is a visual conference between two or more individuals in spite of their location, featuring audio and video content communication in real time.

WeChat: It is a messaging app where you can only consider region and ethnicity.

5.9: Self-Assessment Questions

1. Discuss various roles of technology in business communication.
2. Concentrate on the effects of technology in business communication.
3. What are the advantages of technology in business communication?
4. Mention various advantages of using email.
5. Distinguish between text messaging and instant messaging.

6. State the advantages of instant messaging in business communication.
7. Discuss the benefits of video conferencing.
8. Describe various social networking sites in business communication.
9. Discuss the strategic importance of e-communication.
10. Mention various disadvantages of using email.

Chapter-6

Technical Proposals

Contents

6.1: Learning Objectives

After studying the chapter, you will understand

- The basic concept of technical writing and its importance in business.
- Next, we have thoroughly discussed on which situations, it is necessary to place a proposal.
- The main aims of technical proposal have been summarized.

- The prime functions of the 'Proposal' have been discussed with references.
- Various types of 'proposals' have been addressed.
- The elements of a proposal like Executive Summary, Technical Section, Management Section, Cost Estimate, etc. have been clarified.
- The contents of 'proposals' have been vividly described with a model format.
- Lastly useful writing tips have been provided to prepare a 'Technical Proposal'.

6.2: Introduction

A professional person has to face various situations where it is deemed necessary to prepare technical documents. The technical documents could range from reports, letters, notices, and memos. On the basis of situations, it is indispensable to put the technical proposals. If someone wants to set up a college under the affiliation of a University; he/she needs to create a 'project proposal 'and submit to the University for approval. Likewise, if a company thinks to merge with other company, it is necessary to prepare the reports comprising of the existing company's financial position, infrastructural facilities, manpower planning and objectives of company and submit the proposals.

Thus, we can say that a 'technical proposal' is written by someone who needs to sort out a technical, management or business problem or needs to implement new ideas to enhance proficiency and productivity in various professional operations. Proposals have important role in business growth and professional relationships.

6.3: Purpose

There are various purposes to write a 'technical Proposal' which are given below:

1. The main aim of "technical proposals" is to create something that requires a good understanding of technical knowledge and skills.

2. The sales proposals help to assess and improve the products or services to fulfill the demands of the market.

3. It also helps to create research proposal where the researcher may plan to do a systematic scientific research encircling theory, procedure or its application. These help to fill the gaps of 'theory' and 'practice' and also academics and industry.

6.4: Functions

Proposals are considered as key documents of any project. Naturally it is significant to know the proposal document and ensure the good quality to serve. The main functions of the 'Technical Proposals' are given below:

1. **Indicator:** Technical proposals serve as a pointer of the growth of an organization.

2. **Strategic Collaboration:** The proposals help to invite other companies or industries for strategic alliances, joint venture, acquisition, and merger. These also help in securing technology partnership, event sponsorship.

3. **Fund Raising:** The proposals are prepared to convince the contributor about the need. The proper approach will attain a good result and ensure accountability.

4. **Design:** Good quality outcomes mainly depend upon quality project design. A 'project proposal' is used to represent an appropriate design which includes of activity and budget.

5. **Implementation:** 'Technical Proposal' serves as a key management tool to implement of successful projects. It should have a vibrant logic with adequate description of activities.

6. **Accountability:** The 'Technical Proposal' is accountable for its delivery. So, it is desirable to prepare a 'proposal' which is feasible as well as achievable.

6.5: Importance

The Technical Proposals play a significant role in current business world and in academic arena. The main importance of technical proposals can be described below:

1. As the proposals present the business ideas effectively, they help the business unit by improving its products and services.
2. Proposals serve as an 'indicator' for the growth of an organization.
3. Technical proposals help to invite other companies for strategic alliances, joint ventures, acquisitions and mergers.
4. Proposals help in gaining partnership, fundraising, sponsorship, tenders, or inviting others for participating in an event.
5. Successful proposals usually ensure financial gain.
6. Research proposals help in creating new methods and procedures.

6.6: Types

The 'Proposals' have been categorized into two segments- 'solicited' and 'unsolicited'.

Solicited Proposals: A 'solicited proposal' is written in response to the request put by a client. In many cases, a standard format of 'Proposal' is provided to submit. Government agencies use to ask such type of proposal from the suppliers. 'Solicited proposals' are generally easier to write as they have given clear guidelines.

Unsolicited Proposals: These are written without any request. These are in more detailed and will draw the attention of the receiver. These are based on an objective assessment of a situation or condition. For instance, a senior manager identifying a problem wants to put his/ her proposal on how to handle it, may submit an unsolicited proposal.

6.7: Contents

No specific guidelines are given for technical proposals. A content of a proposal is determined on the basis of its requirement. Certain elements are found common in all most all proposals. These elements are grouped in certain sections usually sequenced as below:

I Executive Summary

II Technical Section

III Management Section

IV Cost Estimation

Let us briefly describe each section:

I Executive Summary

The summary is basically the full proposal in a nut shell. It is frequently circulated to the authority for taking a decision. A well written, comprehensive, and concise summary will be accepted.

A good 'executive summary' can be framed with five paragraphs which are as follows:

1st Paragraph: To project an outline of the business: Here, you have to mention the 'name' and 'nature' of your business.

2nd Paragraph: To focus about the target market, competitor, and the marketing strategy.

3rd Paragraph: To give an overview of operational highlights such as the location of set up the office premises, sole proprietor or partnership business.

4th Paragraph: Here, you have to project the sales forecasting. You need to calculate the 'Break Even Point', and provide information of earning a profit.

5th Paragraph: Here, you have to mention the investment needs clearly. It should align with your business projections.

II Technical Section

This is the most vital section of the 'proposal'. So, the drafting is required with great care and accuracy. It has to be written stepwise which are as follows:

- In first step, it is recommended to describe the nature of the problem, its background, and the relevant works already been done in this field.
- In next step, the proposed work has to be defined in a systematic manner. It is important to mention the scope of the study and limitations. It is also essential to mention the methodology to be applied for the project mentioning the results.
- Lastly, a plan of action has to be narrated clearly. It is necessary in some cases to underscore some segment of the proposal which is unique in design, process or application. Also to focus the theoretical, technical and operational aspects that would accrue on the execution of the proposal. Very often, it is required to propose the development of any new components which has to justify.

III Management Section

It should clearly indicate how the project would be completed. The recipient would obviously be interested in assessing whether the project will be completed by the efficient manpower and the basic resources to implement it.

In executing a proposal it is necessary to engage some competent person. It is equally important to give a short description about their educational qualifications, professional experience, etc.

It is also important to mention the existing facilities e.g. laboratory equipment, plant lay out, etc. and the additional facilities required for this project.

IV Cost Estimation

In solicited proposals, it is necessary to put the amount and type of cost data. In the case of 'unsolicited proposals', it is suggested to add all the items of anticipated expenditure which is realistic, accurate, and complete. Most technical proposals contain the cost analysis of the items mentioned below:

- Machinery and equipment
- Salary of the technical person
- Travel allowances
- Contingencies
- Outside consultancy services

6.8: Format

There are various types of technical proposals. As a reference, a 'sample format' is given below:

Project Title

By

Proposer's name

Design

Name of the organization

Month & Year of submission

ation

Organization's name

Month & Year of submission

Title of the project

By

Name of the Proposer

Designation

1.0 Executive Summary

1.1 Project Title

1.2 'Name' and 'Designation' of the Proposer

1.3 Address of the Proposer/(s)

1.4 Organization's name

1.5 Estimated time for commencement of the 'project 'on receipt of approval

1.6 Duration of the project

1.7 Amount of the money required : (To give year wise back up)

1.8 Summary of the 'Proposal' (Containing technical details in about 200 words)

2.0Table of Contents

3. 0 Technical Background

3.1 To identify the problem with a justification to carry out the project

3.2 To provide technical knowhow about the proposed work

3.2.1 Theoretical aspects

3.2.2 Previous results

3.2.3 Model Framework

3.2.4 Implications of the project with its viability

3.2.5 Identify and mention the critical needs

4.0 Technical Approach

4.1 To identify the specific objectives

4.2 Work Plan

4.2.1 Tasks to meet the objectives

4.2.2 Project Schedule

4.2.3 Estimated Costs (To determine costs involved in each task including of labour cost)

5.0 Capabilities

5.1: To describe the team management structure with the list comprises of qualifications and experience of team members.

5.2: To Identify the equipment to be used and/or purchased to complete the project. It is necessary to clearly specify the required equipment for the project

6.0: Benefits of the Proposed Project

In this section, it should clearly identify the benefits of undertaking the proposed work. These are included of economic benefits, environmental benefits or societal benefits.

7.0 Anticipated Impact on Environment

In this section, it should clearly identify the adverse environmental impacts arising due to this work. The impacts like chemical hazards which require subsequent disposal/ emission of poisonous substances during the operation.

8.0 Nomenclature

It is a devising of names for things. The nomenclature list should be in alphabetical order (capital letter first and then lower case letters) followed by any Greek symbols identified with headings.

9.0 References

While writing a proposal, it is required to gather all the necessary information from various sources like: books, journals, reports, magazines or websites. So, it is important for a proposer to give complete information about the sources from where he/she has referred to his/her proposal.

10.0 Appendices:

A technical article may contain appendices. An appendix contains supporting documents like materials or data that kept separate from the main body of the article to avoid interrupting the line of development of the article.

6.9: Useful Writing Tips to Prepare a Technical Proposal

To create a good 'technical proposal', you have to devote your time and effort. Try to prepare the proposal in a simple and well-formatted manner. A few useful tips have been given which would help to create your technical proposal.

1. Process must be followed while writing a proposal.
2. The 'project proposal' should be 'well defined', 'attainable,' and 'measurable'. You have to ensure that the proposal can be offered in a nice manner.
3. While writing a proposal, imagine that you are presenting it in front of your clients. Satisfy their needs with your real deliverable.

6.10: Glossary

Appendices: A technical article may contain appendices. An appendix contains supporting documents like materials or data that kept separate from the main body of the article to avoid interrupting the line of development of the article.

Executive Summary: It is often circulated to the concerned authority for taking a decision. A well written, comprehensive, and concise summary would be convincing for accepting the project.

Nomenclature: It is a devising of names for things. The nomenclature list should be in alphabetical order (capital letter first and then lower case letters) followed by any Greek symbols identified with headings.

Solicited Proposals: These are written in response to a specific request from a client. In many cases, a standard format is provided to the parties to submit their proposals.

Technical Proposals: It is written by someone who needs to sort out a technical, management or business problem or needs to implement new ideas to enhance productivity in various professional operations. Proposals have important role in business growth and professional relationships.

Unsolicited Proposals: They are more detailed and should draw the attention of the receiver. These proposals are based on an objective assessment of a situation or condition by an individual or a firm.

6.11: Questions

Section "A": Conceptual Questions

1. Write Short notes on the following:

   (a) Nature and significance of 'Technical Proposals'.

   (b) 'Solicited' and 'Unsolicited' Proposals

2. What do you understand by the term 'Executive Summary'? Mention the main elements which are included to prepare an 'Executive Summary'.

3. What are the main contents of 'Technical Proposal'? Discuss with suitable examples.

4. "A proposal is a combination of marketing and technical skill". Comment the statement and illustrate your views with the help of appropriate examples.

Section "B": Assignments

5. You are the Vice President of operations for a chain of Restaurants. You are planning to open a new outlet at Jaipur- on Jaipur -Delhi Highway. You need to prepare a technical proposal for this purpose to be submitted. Now you prepare a draft of this proposal. Your proposal should consist of the following elements:

i) Title Page

ii) Introduction

iii) Technical Section

iv) Management section

v) Cost Estimate

6. Global University is the name of a University that has recently been established in Durgapur, West Bengal. The university has recently sought proposals from professionals who can help it set up a computer lab on its campus. Assuming you are an expert in the field. Draft a proposal to be sent to the Registrar of the University.

Chapter-7

Technical Articles

Contents

7.0: Learning Objectives

After studying the chapter you will get a general idea of

- The conception of technical articles and its' nature and significance.
- Next, we have briefly described diverse types of technical articles with the reference to journal articles, conference papers, review articles, and research article.
- Then we have discussed the structure of a technical article which includes title, author's details, abstract, introduction, methodology, research findings, discussion, conclusion, appendices, references, and bibliography. A short description

of each of these has been given by putting suitable examples.

- Next, we have discussed the effective writing strategies for a research article with the necessary steps which will help to plan, organize, and write the article systematically.
- We have concluded the chapter by putting the glossaries of each item.

7.1: Introduction

A technical article is a written composition which describes, discuss, or analyse a systematic investigation towards increasing the sum of knowledge on a particular field. It transfers new research and findings to other scientists or researchers in the field by providing a systematic account of results of some survey, research, fieldwork, etc. Technical articles differ from general articles in style, presentation, and objectives. A general article may follow any form and pattern whereas a technical article is highly formalised in structure. Technocrats and professionals need to have good technical and writing skills for preparation of report, documentation, or presentation.

7.2: Nature and Significance

Technical articles are useful to all fields of science, technology, humanities, and social sciences. All these contribute to the existing domain of knowledge. Writing a technical article and published in a reputed journal, or presented in a seminar or conference is a challenging issue.

A technical article is an important form of technical communication. It is essential to know how to write a technical article in order to contribute to one's area of interest and specialization. The skill of writing helps in achieving academic and occupational goals. Also, it helps the author's presence to the professional world which will give a high degree of professional satisfaction and help in career development. Technical articles involve the use of technical vocabulary, specific terminology, graphics, aids, and a particular style of writing. Moreover, at the time of writing a technical article, the conventions of the particular discipline need to be followed.

7.3: Types

Technical articles can be classified as journal articles, conference papers, review articles, and research article.

1) **Journal Article:** A journal article is the communication of technical information in a structured form according to the format given by the publishing authority. Most of the reputed journal follows a certain style and format which are being followed by a technical writer. Generally the writing instruction that may follow the guidelines about the preparation of text, organization, length, referencing system and use of symbols, abbreviation illustrations and so on.

2) **Conference Paper:** This paper has been presented by the author in a seminar, conference or workshop. As it is written form of technical presentation, it follows the pattern in which it has been prescribed before the audience. It can be published in the "proceedings" of the conference in which it has been presented. However, the academic value of a conference paper is generally less than that of a journal article.

3) **Review Article:** A review article is an evaluation and analysis of published work on a particular topic. The focal intention of a review article is to evaluate a published work to determine its academic value and research potential.

4) **Research Article:** It is based on unique research carried out by the authors. It may be the outcome of a particular research project carried out by the author. The research may be conducted in the field or in the laboratory. Usually it is theory based or a part of action research to develop certain methods, equipment, procedures, systems, etc. The key reason of research article is to add to the existing knowledge, understanding, and to cope with particular

topics. To achieve its objectives it could be either published in a journal or presented in a conference.

The various types of research articles can be explained through the following table.

Table 7.1: Types and Description of Research Article

Types	Description
Journal Articles	Communication of technical information in a structured form as per the instructions given to the authors for publication in the particular journal.
Conference Papers	The written form of a technical presentation that would be presented in a seminar, conference, or workshop.
Review Articles	Evaluation and analysis of published work
Research Articles	An objective description and discussion based on a research project

7.4: Structure of a Technical Article

Research papers are generally formalised structure. They usually follow fixed pattern to ensure objectivity. Though, we need to choose and arrange components of a research paper as per the requirement of an organization or the convention of a journal. The components of technical articles are: Title, Author's details, Abstract, Introduction, Methodology, Research findings, Discussion, Conclusion, Appendices, References, and Bibliography. Let us discuss of each of these elements.

1. Title: All technical articles begin with a title. Title is the first component that meets the reader's eye. The title of a technical article is usually a long phase that contains keywords and indicates the content of the article. Therefore, the title of a research article should be informative, specific, and comprehensive. We need to begin the title with the content words, such as nouns, verbs, adjectives, adverbs, gerunds, etc., with a capital letter and need not choose capital letters for beginning function words such as articles, conjunctions, and prepositions. Let us look at the title worded below:

The impact of an Organization's Culture on Organizational Commitment to Job Satisfaction and Employee Performance: A Study on the Frontline Hotel Employees of India

2. Author's Details: This is the second element of a technical article. Generally, it includes the name of the author followed by institutional affiliation. When a research paper is jointly authored by two or more authors, the names of all the authors are listed with their respective affiliations are separately highlighted. Take a look at how to arrange such details about the author of a research article:

The Impact of an Organization's Culture on Organizational Commitment to Job Satisfaction and Employee Performance: A Study on the Frontline Hotel Employees of India

by
Dr Adrita
Assistant Professor
IIM, Kolkata

3. Abstract: This is the most significant elements of a technical article. The abstract of a paper captures the essence of the research. There are two kinds of abstracts, that is, descriptive and informative. The descriptive abstract talks about the article and briefly states what the article contains while the informative abstract summarizes the essential information in the article focusing on key facts, findings, observations, results, conclusions, and recommendations. Informative abstracts are more comprehensive and self explanatory than descriptive abstract. An effectively written abstract has the following key features:

i) It states the objective of the research.

ii) It provides a brief description of the experiment conducted during the research.

iii) It mentions the main outcomes of the research discussed in detail in the research paper.

iv) The facts, observations, and results reported in an abstract are consistent with the details of the research paper.

v) The significance of the research should be mentioned.

vi) As regards its style, an abstract is written scientifically and in a clear and objective manner.

vii) It is written in one single paragraph.

3. Introduction: The main part of a technical article generally begins with an introduction and introduces the reader to the topic or the research work under discussion. This section helps the reader to comprehend the article as it includes facts that the reader should know to comprehend the discussion and analysis that follow. In a good article, introduction may include the following elements.

Table 7.2: Elements and Description of Introduction

Elements	Description
Background	An objective description of the background of the problem, or events and conditions that led to the problem under discussion
Research status	The status of the research related to the problem, and the need of the present research
Purpose	Aims and objectives of the research or investigation
Methods	Methods or procedures to conduct the research work and the justification for using specific methods of investigation
Significance	Researcher briefly highlights the major findings of the research and emphasizes their significance and relevance as a valuable contribution to the existing body of knowledge

4. Methodology: While writing a technical article, it is necessary to mention the methods and materials to be applied to conduct the investigation. The professional value of an investigation largely depends upon the using appropriate method. In order to establish the validity of the findings, the materials and methods used need to be described along with the justification for using them. This may involve the research design, research procedures, kind of data, data collection procedure, and the criteria of survey.

5. Discussion on Results and Findings: Constituting a detailed analysis of the major findings and results of the research, the discussion section of a paper is its' most voluminous part. This part of a research article presents to the reader all the main ideas of the research and expands it with the requisite details and explanation. It also provides a clear and convincing analysis of the research undertaken. This section brings into view the causes, implications of all results and findings of the research. By referring to the relevant researches in a particular field of study; it also establishes a link between the research conducted and the existing body of knowledge. While writing the discussion of a research paper, we need to keep the following criteria in our mind:

i) To divide the entire text of the discussion into different headings and subheadings.

ii) Arrange the ideas in order of importance

iii) Use figures, tables to provide proper information related to the subject.

iv) Analyse the problem by emphasizing the relevance of the research.

v) Discuss in detail all the major findings and results of the research in a clear and precise manner.

vi) To give focus more on the discussion of facts, findings, and results of the research rather than on imagination.

vii) Help the reader conceptualize the problem and carry on the discussion aiming to a solution.

viii) Importance should be given to the research rather than the researcher. Write from the perspective of the research, e.g. '...the research establishes...', '...the facts indicate...' etc.

ix) It is more appropriate to write in such a tone and manner that suits the grace of the researcher, e.g.'...It seems the suggested method can help to resolve ...'the experiment brings to the fore the utility of ...', etc

6. **Conclusions:** This section concludes the article by summarising the important highlights of the article. It is generally concise and infers in a factual and logical manner. To write a conclusion the following points to take into consideration:

i) To keep the conclusion precise, realistic and brief.

ii) A conclusion derives its observations from the main discussion of the research; therefore, avoid adding anything new in this stage.

iii) Maintain consistency in the objective listed in the introduction, the facts established in the discussion and the inferences derived in the conclusion section of the research paper.

iv) Mention the need of further study, if required.

7. **Appendices:** A technical article may contain appendices. An appendix contains supporting documents like materials or data that kept separate from the main body of the article to avoid interrupting the line of development of the article.

8. **Bibliography:** A research paper often concludes with a bibliography that provides a complete list of all the books, journals, newspaper, magazines, and websites referred by

the researchers. It may use the referring method approved in the particular discipline to which the article belongs. Whatever forms of referring is used; the author has to provide complete information about the sources he/she has referred to his/her writing.

The following are the guidelines to organize references:

Sources	Referring method	Example
Book	To include author's title and publication information. The name of the author begins with the surname. The title should be italics. Publication information includes the place of publication, the name of the publisher, the year of publication and volume, issue and page number	Southall, JPC, *Mirrors, Prisms and lences*, 3d ed. New York: The Macmillan Company,1936
Reports	To include name of the report writer/writers, title of the report, place of publication, publisher's name, year of publication	Srivastava, BK, *A Project Proposed on A Study of Quantification and their Weightages for Parameters of Environmental Impact Assessment*, Varanasi Institute of Technology, Banaras Hindu University, May 2000
Journal	To mention the name of the author, article, journal, volume no, issue no, page no and date of issue. Name of the article is within inverted commas while the name of the journal is in italics.	David Stewart, "Description, Materiality and Survey Research : Some Lessons from Craft", *Journal of Public Policy and Marketing*, September 1995):15-28
Magazine / News paper	It includes the name of the author, article/paper, newspaper and date of publication. A comma is used to separate each detail of the entry. The name of the article is written within inverted commas while the name of the magazine or newspaper is in italics.	Rajlaxmi Bhattacharya," Mission Impossible", *The Telegraph Magazine*,26(April 1998)
Conference proceedings	It includes the author's name along with topics publication details of proceedings Place, date, year There should not be any italic portion.	V M S R Murthy, A K Ghosh, "Planning for faster drivage rate with road headers in Indian Long wall Mines: A field investigation". Proc. of the 6th Symposium on Mines Planning and Equipment selection, Ostrava Czech Republic, September 3-6, 1997.
Internet	It may include the author's name (if any) ,the title of the document, location of the information and web address	"Tikvart J A,. " Particulate matter from surface coal mining',1991(http://www.epa.gov/ttn/scram/guidance/mch/cfym48.txt
Dissertation	It includes name, year, title, university	Mcdonalds, A (1991), Practical dissertation title (Un published doctoral dissertation) University of Florida

7.5: Writing Strategy

A technical article is the formal, structured, and short presentation of technical information. It is necessary to adopt effective writing strategies to deliver the article properly. The following steps will help to plan, organize, and write the article systematically.

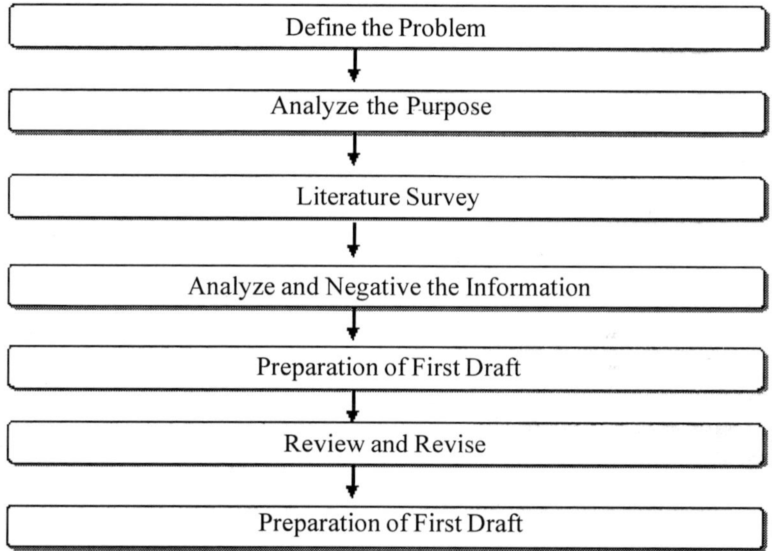

Let us shortly describe each of them.

1. Define the Problem: Planning for an article should start with defining the problem. This is the first step of any systematic investigation. Here, the author needs to analyze the problem that he/ she wants to discuss objectively. Defining the problem will also help in deciding the approach, content, and methodology. The problem may be written down in the form of a statement. This problem statement could be the guiding principles for writing the articles.

2. Analyze the Purpose: The purpose of writing an article needs to be defined in order to write a result oriented paper. Defining and analyzing the purpose will help in making the article relevant and effective. As the aim of the research needs to be mentioned in the abstract of the article, the objective of the research should be written in a sentence.

3. Literature Survey: It is the essential segment of any credible research. Survey of existing literature is essential to be informed about the latest research in the area of investigation, which helps to give a theoretical foundation to the article. It also helps correlate the article to the mainstream of scientific literature in the field.

4. Analyze and Organize the Information: Once the problem and purpose have been defined, literature surveyed, and information gathered, the writer needs to analyze and organize the material. The writer may organize the information by using an appropriate pattern to arrange the information.

5. Preparation of First Draft: Once an outline has been prepared and the organizational pattern of the article has been decided, the first draft may be written. While writing the first draft, the author needs to ensure that his/her article is divided into reasonable sections with appropriate headings and sub headings.

6. Review and Revise: Once the rough draft of the article has been written, it should be reviewed, edited, and revised to improve the quality of its content and presentation. Reviewing involves the process of analyzing whether the article achieved its purpose whereas editing involves correcting its style, grammar, spelling, and punctuation.

7. Preparation of Final Draft: Once the rough draft of the article has been reviewed and revised, the final draft can be written. While writing the final draft the following points should be taken care of:

- Effective and meaningful sentence and clear paragraph should be used.
- Principles of technical style should be taken care of
- The article should be objective, impersonal, clear and concise
- Appropriate linking devices should be used.

7.6: Summary

A technical article is a written composition which describes, discuss, or analyze a systematic investigation towards increasing the sum of knowledge on a particular field. Technical articles are useful to all fields of science, technology, humanities, and social sciences. Technical articles can be classified as journal articles, conference papers, review articles, and research article. The components of technical articles are: Title, Author's details, Abstract, Introduction, Methodology, Research findings, Discussion, Conclusion, Appendices, References, and Bibliography.A technical article is the formal, structured, and short presentation of technical information. It is necessary to adopt effective writing strategies to deliver the article properly.

7.7: Glossary

Abstract: The abstract is the most important elements of a technical article. The abstract of a paper captures the essence of the research. It summarizes the essential information in the article focusing on key facts, findings, observations, results, conclusions, and recommendations.

Appendices: A technical article may contain appendices. It contains supporting documents like materials or data that kept separate from the main body of the article to avoid interrupting the line of development of the article.

Bibliography: A research paper often concludes with a bibliography that provides a complete list of all the books, journals, newspaper, magazines, and websites referred by the researchers.

Conclusions: This section concludes the article by summarising the significant highlights of the article. It is generally concise and infers in a factual and logical manner.

Conference Paper: It is the text of a paper that the author has presented in a seminar, conference or workshop.

Introduction: It is the main part of a technical article and introduces the reader to the topic or the research work under discussion. This section helps the reader to understand the article as it includes facts that the reader must know to comprehend the discussion and analysis that follow.

Journal Article: A journal article is the communication of technical information in a structured form as per the format given by the publishing authority.

Literature Survey: It is the essential segment of any credible research. Survey of existing literature is essential to be informed about the latest research in the area of investigation, which helps to give a theoretical foundation to the article.

Methodology: While writing a technical article, it is necessary to mention the methods and materials to be used to conduct the investigation. In order to establish the validity of the findings, the materials and methods used need to be described along with the justification for using them. This may involve the research design, research procedures, kind of data, data collection procedure, and the criteria of survey.

Reference: It is the complete information about the sources from where the author has referred to his/her writing.

Research Article: It is based on original research carried out by the authors.

Review Article: A review article is an evaluation and analysis of published work on a particular topic.

Technical Article: It is basically a written composition which describes, discuss, or analyze a systematic investigation towards increasing the sum of knowledge on a specific field.

Title: It is the first component of all technical articles.

7.8: Conceptual Questions

1. Write brief notes on the following:

a) Conference Papers

b) Research Article

c) Title of a Technical Article

d) Introduction of a Technical Article

e) Methodology in Technical Articles

2. Explain the following statements into one paragraph each.

a) Technical articles are essential to all fields of science and technology.

b) All technical articles should be objective and factual.

c) The abstract is the most important element of a technical article.

3. 'Research paper is more than narration of facts and accumulation of data or direct quotations.' Do you agree to the statement? Elucidate your answer in about 400 words.

4. Briefly discuss the writing strategies for a research article.

5. Mention the different types and description of research article.

6. Provide a suitable title for a research paper from your domain and develop a paper by using the following elements

i) Title
ii) Abstract
iii) Introduction
iv) Mythology
v) Results
vi) Discussion
vii) Conclusion
viii) References

Chapter-8

Group Discussion

Contents

8.0: Learning Outcomes

The chapter will give a general idea of

- Group Discussion: Concept, importance.
- We have briefly described different types of GD with examples

- Also we have discussed on the typical characteristics of group discussion
- Next, we have discussed Group Interaction Strategies with the help of some examples
- We have discussed the prime areas of evaluation
- Finally the strategies for a GD leader have been discussed which is very relevant.
- We have finished the chapter by putting the glossaries of each item.

8.1: Introduction

We often find people discussing various issues like personal, social, economic, political or current happenings. These discussions might be formal and informal. Informal private discussions can take place at home, at a recreation club, at a restaurant, at a canteen or even in a coffee shop. On the contrary formal discussion may take place at an office, at a conference hall, at a meeting room, or at a recruitment centre. It is obvious that we involve in discussion to create a better ideas on key issues

Let us now try to make out the term "Group Discussion': It is referred as "an unrestrained situation that permits its participants to express their views and opinions". It is fundamentally "an interactive oral process". The exchange of thoughts ideas can take place through verbal communication. The GD participants use to listen of version of others and give their own views.

GD is a methodical 'oral exchange of information', thought and opinion about a specific topic, issue, problem. This method is used by an organization to measure the candidate's personality traits and skills. A suitable example of a GD is a football match where all players pass the ball to their fellow team players with an aim to score goal. The team which has better coordination and skills wins the game and so is the case with GD. In group discussions the members have to interpret, analyse and argue critically based on the topic.

GD is a goal oriented activities. The goals or objectives of a discussion are normally decided before the discussion gets started.

To conclude we may define GD as "a form of organized and purposeful oral process for developing information and understanding essential for decision making or problem solving".

8.2: Importance of Group Discussion

To attain the professional success the capability to join in GD is essential for a candidate. Whether a student, an autocrat, or an executive, one must need of group discussion skills. A student may have to participate in scholastic discussions, group deliberation, interactive class room sessions, or to get selected for a professional course. Job seekers may face a GD as a partial requirement of his/her selection process. Professionals in different fields also engaged in professional meetings and discussions. These situations require a capacity to make a significant contribution to group deliberation and facilitate the group in certain decision making factor/(s)

Now days, the importance of group discussion has increased due to

(a) Solving Problems

(b) Decision Taking

(c) Personality Assignment

Presently all most all the companies and institutions, GD aids in problem solves and decision making. When a problematic situation arises, the concerned people use to discuss to resolve the problem. They exchange their views to recognize the problem with possible solutions. Thus the alternative solutions are discussed and analysed to decide the best option.

'Group discussion' is a technique for personality assignment which is necessary for a candidate for job selection or to be admitted in professional courses. Generally, six - eight members are formed a group and given a definite topic to discuss. The topics vary from either a problem or may be an opinion or related to a case study. The panel of selection body evaluate the different skills reflected by the candidates like leadership quality or the quality to analyse a critical situation and work upon it.

It is essential to organise a GD effectively. The participants should have the power to convince the other group members, with self confidence with leadership qualities. They should possess skill to take proper initiatives during a discussion. They need to present their personal views in a logical way.

8.3: Participants and Duration

In a formal GD group, there are generally six to fifteen members. They are asked to take a seat in a circular, semi-circular or U –shaped sitting style. The participants are given fifteen to forty minutes to discuss upon a certain topic.

78.4: Types

Generally GDs are of two types - Topic –based and Case based

GD on topic –based are divided in three types:

i) Factual Topics

ii) Abstract –Topics

iii) Controversial Topics

Types of GD can be shown in the following diagram

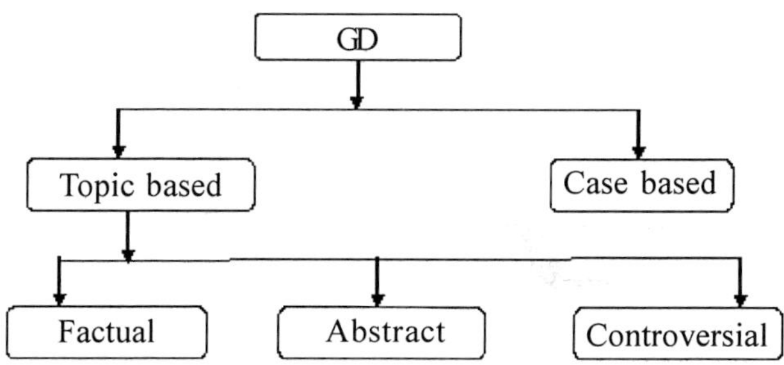

Fig: 8.1 Types of GDs

Factual Topics

Mostly groups are given factual topics. They are generally related with the current socio economic facts or based on environmental issues. For example, growth of Indian Tourism or Women's empowerment is the examples factual topics

Abstract –Topics

These are given at the higher level and are usually in tangible in nature. These need to approach with innovativeness and lateral thinking. The topics like: Money makes you poor, High Ambition invites frustration etc are the examples of abstract topics.

Controversial Topics:

These are controversial in nature. Participants are forced to give different opinion. These types of topics are generally given to assess the maturity level of the participants. For example, a candidate may be instructed to talk about debatable issues like "Reservation should be abolished in India" or "Women are Unfit for Defence Services."

Case Based

The topics are based on real life situations. Usually these are involve with specific problems which are to be determined. These topics are not well defined with specific correct or wrong answer rather it dependent upon the approaches of participants to the solutions.

8.5: Characteristics

Effective GD achieves group goals and aids in decision making. It is necessary to be familiar with the characteristics that make a GD successful which are described below:

Agreement on Group Goals: An effective group discussion starts with a purpose, which is shared and by the participates of the group. It helps them to focus on the topics and build them more active in realising the group goals. They can smoothly work from general purpose to specific goals. Moreover, the agreement on group goals brings clarity and provides direction to group.

Goal Centric Interaction: Successful discussions motivate group members to have goal oriented interaction. Effective GD members are not only conscious about group goals but also work towards the attainment of these goals.

Agreement on Procedures: Participants of a successful GD develop procedure s to guide them. To attain the group goals, they may develop the norms of interaction. They decide the factors like how the individual views will be presented, how an exchange of views will be given, and how they will arrive to a group agreement.

Cooperative and Friendly Atmosphere: An important characteristic of successful GDs is to create a supportive and affable atmosphere where disagreement does exist but it will not direct to major conflicts. Members extend their cooperation as they understand and appreciate different points of views and aim to pool them together to develop group harmony.

Equal Distribution of Participation: A successful group discussion ensures an equal distribution of participation by all. All the members are important and none is allowed to dominate the discussion.

Applications of Effective Communication Techniques: The successful group discussions are mainly depend on the exercise of communication techniques. Effective GD members keep the channels of communication open and speak clearly and precisely using simple words, short sentences, correct articulation.

Shared Leadership: Usually there is a formal GD leader. The leadership functions are shared and performed by the various group members.

8.6: Group Interaction Strategies

Group interaction is a forum that provides a platform for interaction. Proper interaction is possible only if the every participant contributes his/her understanding level on the topic for discussion. To ensure the top performance it is significant to know the techniques to exchange opinions and suggestions in group discussions.

Exchanging Opinion: Exchanging opinions during GDs include asking for opinions, giving opinions, supporting opinions, balancing point of views, agreeing and disagreeing.

i) Asking for opinions: You may ask one person to give his/her opinion on any point. This can be explained with the following table:

Table: 8.1

Directed at one person	*Directed at a group of people*
What is your opinion about this?	Does anyone have strong views on this?
What do you think about this?	What is the general views on this?
What do you feel about this?	Does anybody have any comments to make?
Do you have anything to say	Does anybody have anything to say?

ii) Giving Opinion: During a group discussion the participants have to give their opinion about the subject being discussed. The members of the group need to react to the views given by the other members. You may express an opinion in a strong way neutral way or tentative way. It is important to make other members conscious of your opinion. It can be explained with the help of the following table:

Table: 8.2

Strong opinion	*Neutral opinion*	*Tentative opinion*
I'm pretty sure that ...	I believe that...	It seems to me that...
I'm sure that...	According to me...	I'm inclined to think that...
I strongly believe that...	I feel that...	It appears to me that...
I'm quite convinced that...	Personally I think ...	I might accept the view that...

iii) Supporting your opinion: To make your views acceptable to others

To make your views acceptable to other participants, it is necessary to support them with logic, facts, examples, illustrations, or arguments. This is illustrated by the following examples:

- I'm convinced that our company must open new braches because our business has explained.
- I'm sure that reducing the prices will improve our sales.
- I think, we should go ahead with this project as it will help us to create brand name.

iv) Balancing Point of View: To be reasonable and rational, GD participants may have to balance points of view by trying to view the both sides of a given opinion. They need to balance advantages and disadvantages. A few examples are listed below:

Of course, reducing the prices of our car will help us clear the old stock and improve our sales but it will adversely affect the company profits

Exchanging Suggestions: During a GD, it is necessary for a participant to take suggestions of other participants to conduct the discussion. It can be explained with the following table:

Table: 8.3

Directed at one person	*Directed at the people in the group*
What do you suggest?	Any suggestions?
What should we do?	I'd like to have some of your recommendations.
What do you recommend?	Do any of you want to make any suggestion or recommendation?

Accepting/ Rejecting Proposals: While discussing a problem, or a case, proposals put forward by other group members may be accepted or rejected. The examples are shown below:

Table: 8.3

Strong support/rejections	*Weak Support/rejections*
I think, it is the best solution	It appears to be a good plan
That's a great idea.	OK
It is an excellent idea	It may be tried...
I'm completely in favour of that	Fine
It is not possible to accept that	I'm sorry I can't accept that
It is not feasible	I'm sorry but it is not feasible

8.7: Assessment Through GD

GD has emerged as effective and powerful techniques for evaluating personality traits of a candidate for job selection or to get admitted in professional courses. There are mainly four areas of evaluation:

1. Subject Knowledge
2. Oral Communication Skills
3. Leadership Skills
4. Team Management Skills

1. Subject Knowledge: This may be considered as a prime requirement of effective participation in a GD.Participants needs to have fair subject knowledge. People with subject knowledge in depth are always sought by dynamic working environment. Subject knowledge also implies the capability to analyse facts or information in a methodical way to correlate them with personal experience and exposure. It is the capability to analyse existing knowledge and assimilate new ideas can generate innovative ideas. During selection of group discussion, participants are likely to analyse the topic and give their interpretation of it.

2. Verbal Communication Skills: In a group discussion, the exchange of thoughts and ideas mainly take place through speech. One of the prerequisites of success in GD is the capacity to speak confidently. Actually, a successful GD is mainly depending on the high quality of oral communication. The selection board evaluate the skill of verbal communication of the participants. They assess the verbal skill of the participants with the following qualities which are explained below:

- **Listening Skills:** All the comments put by the participants must be heard. Listening skills are considered as one of the most vital communication skills.
- **Clarity of Expression:** This is the unique art of making your expression cleared to others. It is a matter of fact that clear expression is the reflection of clear thinking. Therefore in a group discussion, it is essential to think clearly and positively.
- **Appropriateness of Language:** While conducting a GD, the judges also evaluate the capability to use appropriate words and expressions. Participants must be certain to communicate their ideas precisely and exactly so that their listener is able to understand without any confusion.
- **Clear Articulation:** The voice quality and clear articulation play a significant role in group discussion. A participant of a GD can make impressed to other participants or selection panel if he/she has an attractive voice quality with fine articulation.

3. Leadership Skills: The success of a candidate in a GD will depend on his/her leadership skill. Self-confidence, motivation, initiative, objectivity, and leadership skills are tremendously helpful to prove one as a "natural leader"

4. Team Management Skills: Apart from other qualities, every participant needs to have the knowledge of team management skills. Participants of the group discussion should know the basics of 'Team Management Skills" to function effectively in a team. The essential skills need to administer a group successfully with the help of positive attitude, adaptability, cooperation coordination etc.

8.8: Leader's Strategies in GD

Group Discussion is a systematic interaction process. The following strategies are to be adopted for effective participation in GD

i) Opening of a GD: Generally there is no specific leader to conduct a GD. Naturally no one is allotted to start the GD. After making announcement of the topic, the other relevant issues are addressed like allotted time, general guidelines and procedures etc. Afterwards the examiner withdraws to the background, use to leave the group completely to carry on the discussion.

To get the GD started, the leader of the group will have to tell the group of its goal and request them to start the discussion. A few examples of the opening lines are listed below:

"Well friends. May I have your attention please? we have been allotted 45 minutes to complete the discussion. So, we need to start the discussion immediately."

"Well friends? I am sure, we are eagerly waiting to start the group discussion and complete it within the given time. Let me remind you that we have only forty minutes to complete the assignments. So, we need to start now."

Once the group discussion is initiated, the GD leader will propose the procedures to be executed during the discussion. The procedures may include time management and individual contributions. It is necessary to follow a plan that includes time for individual speaker to exchange his/her views putting suggestions and giving solutions. While starting the group discussion, the group leader ought to attempt to create an atmosphere in which all members feel free to participate.

ii) Contributing to a GD: The main success of GD is depending on systematic contribution of each and every participant of the group and the members should understand the procedure of reflective thinking. Moreover, contributions must reflect the knowledge and the ability of the GD participants .When a participant makes a contribution, he/she should ensure the following things:

- Relates to what has said earlier by other members
- Focuses on the theme of the discussions
- Deals with the specific point

iii) Imitativeness for Optimal Participation: To make a GD successful the leader must promote optimal participation. With patience and motivation he/she can inspire even the shy and reluctant members to present the views on a given topics. It will not only reflect his/her leadership qualities but also lead discussion to successful conclusion. Leaders may find the following suggestions which would help to carry out a successful GD:

- Encourage each member to give the maximum contribution
- Make all members feel that their contribution is necessary
- When a member makes a contribution, the GD leader may request the non-participating members to comments on it
- The leader has to control the talkative members

iv) Handling Conflicts: The important aspects of a leader are to deal with conflicts. As a group always trends to be heterogeneous and conflict is quite natural. During a group discussion, the group leader may expect the difference of opinion but he/she should not let these conflicts against the basic purpose of a discussion. Although resolution of conflict is a critical task, a leader needs to remember the following guidelines which will help him/her to administer the conflict:

- Maintain a friendly attitude and attempt to generate an atmosphere
- The leader must put an effort to keep away the conflicts between persons and not conflict between ideas.

- The leader needs to offer positive guidance to all participants by making summaries of the discussions.
- The leader must help to establish an attitude of critical objectivity.

iv) Summarizing a Discussion and Closure: The group leader has to ensure that GD ends with positive conclusions within a given time limit. For completion of a group discussion within the fixed time, the leader needs to remind the group and request to reach to a group consensus. He/she should do the following to conclude the discussion:

- Summarise the progress made by the participants
- Indicate the differences that need to resolve.
- Review decisions/suggestions

Once the closure of a discussion is successfully initiated, the group leader may propose the consensus views, if any. The leader must highlight agreed points to indicate the common point of view of the topic.

8.9: Summary

Group Discussion (GD)

It is explained as "a method used by an organization to measure whether a candidate possesses certain personality traits or skills which are desired". The objectives of a GD are normally decided prior to the discussion takes place.

Importance of a GD

Group discussions reflect the important skills for a student, an autocrat, or an executive. The importance of GD has its importance due to its effective role in 'problem solving', 'decision making' and 'personality assignment'.

It is vital to conduct a GD effectively. The members of the group must know the skill to convince the group members with confidence and leadership qualities.

Participants and Duration of GD: In a formal GD, there are 6-15 members in a group. They are given 15-45 minutes to through light on a topic.

Types of GD

Generally GDs are of two types - Topic –based and Case based. Topic –based group discussion are of 3 types: Factual topics, Abstract –topics and Controversial topics

Factual Topics: Mostly groups are given topics which are factual in nature.

Abstract Topics: These are in tangible in nature. These need to approach with innovativeness and lateral thinking. The topics like: Money makes you poor, High Ambition invites frustration etc are the examples of abstract topics.

Controversial Topics: These are controversial in nature.

Case Based: The topics are based on real life situations. Usually these involve with problems which are to be resolved.

Characteristics

It is essential to have the knowledge of the characteristics that make a group discussion successful. They are as follows:

Agreement on group goals: An successful GD starts with a purpose, which is shared and understood by all participants.

Goal Centric Interaction: Successful discussions motivate group members to have goal oriented interaction.

Agreement on Procedures: Participants of a successful GD develop procedure s to guide them.

Cooperative and Friendly Atmosphere: An important characteristic of successful GDs is the presence of a supportive and cordial atmosphere

Equal Distribution of Participation: An equal distribution of participation is required for a group discussion. Each member is important and nobody is allowed to dominate the discussion.

Applications of Communication Techniques: A successful GD mainly depends on an effective use of communication techniques.

Shared Leadership: There is generally a group Leader. The leadership functions are shared and performed by the all members.

Group Interaction Strategies: Group interaction is a forum that provides a platform for interaction.

Exchanging Opinion: Exchanging opinions during GDs include asking for opinions, giving opinions, supporting opinions and balancing the views of the participants.

Areas of Evaluation

The four major areas of evaluation in selection GD:

Subject Knowledge: The GD members should have fair subject knowledge.

Verbal Communication Skill: The participants in a group discussion must possess the communication skill to convince the fellow members.

Listening Skills: All the comments put by the participants must be heard. It includes of

- **Clarity of Expression:** This is the unique art of making your expression clear to your addressees.
- **Appropriateness of Language:** During group discussion the judges also evaluate the capability to use appropriate words and expressions.
- **Clear Articulation:** It plays a significant role in a GD.
- **Leadership Skill:** A candidate's success in a group discussion is depending on the leadership quality of his/

her which include adaptability, self-confidence, motivation, initiative, objectivity

- **Team Management:** GD participants require the knowledge of "Team management skills"

Strategies to be Adopted by a Leader of a GD:

A group discussion is an organized interaction and purposeful oral process. The following strategies are to be adopted

Opening of a GD: In a selection GD, the group is given a specific topic to discuss within the given time.

Contributing to a GD: The attainment of a group discussion depends on systematic contribution by the members.

Imitativeness for Optimal Participation: The success of a group discussion is largely depends on the involvement of every member of the group.. With patience and motivation the leader can inspire even the shy and reluctant members to give their views on a given topics.

Handling Conflicts: During a group discussion, the leader may expect the difference of opinion but he/she should not let these conflicts against the basic goals of a GD.

Summarizing a Discussion and Closure: The group leader of a group discussion has to make sure that it ends with positive conclusions within a given time limit.

8.10: Glossary

Abstract –Topics: These are in tangible in nature and need to approach with innovativeness and lateral thinking.

Controversial Topics: The given topics are generally controversial in nature. Participants are bound to give different opinion. These topics are chosen to judge the maturity level of the participants.

Case Based: These are on the basis of real life situations. Usually these involve with some problems which are to be resolved.

Factual Topics: In a formal GD, the participants are given topics which are factual in nature.

Group Discussion (GD): This is a methodical 'oral exchange of information', thought and opinion about a specific topic, issue and problem.

8.11: Conceptual Questions

1. Define the term "Group discussion" (GD)? Why are these important?

2. Discuss the various types of GDs that are used in the selection procedure.

3. Discuss the qualities of a participant that are evaluated through a GD.

4. Discuss the areas of evaluation through GD.

5. Discuss the main characteristics of a "Group Discussion."

6. State the Group Interaction Strategies with suitable examples.

7. Think and write the opening and closing for the following topics:

    a) Art is better than science

    b) To lead a good life ,one needs to have spiritual awakening

    c) 'Quality' is a myth in India

    d) 'Working mothers' are better than mothers who are just housewives

    e) Smoking advertisements should be banned first before banning smoking itself.

8. Write briefly on the following:

    a) Importance of GD.

b) Group interaction in GD

c) Leadership functions in GD

d) Individual contribution in group discussion

9. Participate in a GD based on a topic. You have been allotted twenty five minutes duration for this discussion. The topic will be provided to you on the spot. You will be given five minutes to organise thoughts before the discussion commence. A pool of topics are listed below: Try to prepare your arguments ,opening, and closing for these topics:

a) Aggression has become a part of life.

b) Life is like a Blank Page

c) Indian media requires to be more accountable

d) The structure of the "Civil Services Examinations" should be changed

e) Sick public sector units should be sold to private companies

f) It is easier to speak than listen

g) Brain drain should be stopped

h) A borderless world is the need of the hour

i) Teachers can easily be replaced by computers in "Higher Education"

j) Mobile phones are necessary evils today

k) Influence of Nepotism in Bollywood Film Industry

Chapter-9

Job Interviews

Contents:

9.0: Learning Objectives

After studying this unit, you will understand

- The concept and meaning of 'job interviews'.
- The process of interviews with the required steps
- Then we have elaborately discussed the characteristics of 'job interviews'.

- The main types of interviews are discussed by putting a few questions.
- Pre-interview preparation techniques ,those are essential for an interview have been discussed
- Then we have explained the employer's expectations from a 'job interview'.
- We have discussed the strategies of giving answers an interviewee
- Some frequently asked questions are reviewed
- A summary of the chapter have been outlined
- Glossary have been provided
- Self-assessment questions are given which is extremely helpful for the students

9.1: Concept, Meaning

Many people get nervous to face an interview. For most job applicants, job interviews are frightening due to the fear of rejection. But we can overcome the fear for attending an interview process by understanding the process.

Interview process is a complex means of assembling related data about a candidate for a specific job, promotion, or making a selection panel. It is a structured mechanism for professional evaluation for employment.

Thus a 'job interview 'provides the best opportunity to examine the relevance of an applicant's knowledge skill and experience. It is also a fact that interview is an effective technique used to select a suitable candidate for a position .It could be either by physically present in meeting or formal conversation over phone or videoconferencing between a candidate and the selection committee or the placement agencies work for the concerned employers.

In the modern technological advanced world job interviews are more challenging as the selection board faces the challenge of getting the suitable person. Naturally they are interested to go for a proper assessment of candidate's personal qualities, depth of knowledge, qualifications, talents etc. However the ask is not easy for any selection committee to judge a candidate's capabilities based on short conversation with the candidate. Therefore, innovative and effective interviewing techniques have been introduced for the proper evaluation of a candidate.

A candidate should possess knowledge, confidence and specking power to attend before an interview board to achieve success. He/she should be acquainted with the various types of interviews, interview formats, and appropriate interviewing strategies and should know how to plan and prepare for a 'job interview', how to reflect self-confidence while answering questions and how to uphold his/her personality and overcome interviewing hazard.

9.2: Process

During an interview process the employer attempts to assess the applicant's suitability for the job. During an interview, the interviewers enquired about his /her experience, style of work etc. The recruiters do not wish for selecting a wrong candidate as a wrong would result in further wastage of time .money and energy on their part. In many reputed companies, therefore you can observe that the process of interviewing is gradually changing with the inclusion of group activities, analysis tasks, presentation, and psychometric tests,

Keeping the above mentioned facts in mind, the candidate should keep his/her resume updated and keep on practicing the frequently asked questions. These simple exercises can be very effective. The processes of interview are broadly divided into three steps:

Step:1: Gather information

Step: 2: Establishing a rapport

Step: 3: Closing Interview

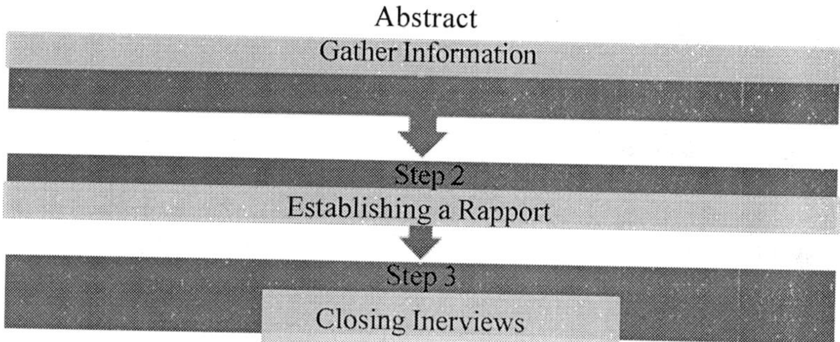

Fig: 9.1. Job Interview Process

Step: 1: Gather Information

At the very beginning, you need to gather the information regarding the companies where you plan to attend the interview. It is deemed necessary to search information about the company, its products, number of employees .its branches, total turnover, work culture, and future plan of your prospective company.

Step: 2: Establishing a Rapport

By obtaining the above information you can build a rapport with the interview board.

Step: 3: Closing Interview

Finally you need to be prepared for the closing interview. It is possible that you might be asked to raise a question. Be ready with one, and think about your concluding remarks when the interviewers tell you that your interview is over. It is suggested to attain the following objectives in the time of closing an interview

1. Clear the fact that you require the job
2. An effort to create a good impression on you
3. Get the offer for the job

9.3: Characteristics

'Job interview' is a prearranged and planed conversation characterized by a defined purpose and some level of informality. There are five aspects of interview like planning. Purpose, conversation, two way interaction and informality. Let us discuss these in some detail

1. Planning: The most job interviews are arranged with a view to achieve effective results. Several factors are decided before conducting an interview such as time, venue, number of section board members and so on. The interviewers may also consider the best ways of opening and concluding interviews. However job interviews are not a mechanical process of asking and getting answers from the interviewees. The interviewer may plan and generate specific questions for each candidate with modifications in the planned interview design.

2. Purpose: An interview is purposefully designed to achieve certain objectives. Most of the organizations invest money and time to conduct interviews to ensure certain correct selections. There may be HR interviews to test the personality of the candidates, technical interviews to judge the subject knowledge, situational interviews to examine the problem solving skills or criterion based interview to test knowledge and abilities of a candidate to find a suitable person Whatever may be the format of an interview for the vacant job, the purpose is predefined.

3. Conversation: A 'job interview' is basically a talk between the recruiters and the applicant where mainly question – answer session is been occurred. As it includes both listening and speaking, the candidate needs to listen actively during an interview process and speak clearly and precisely using simple words, correct articulation with appropriate pronunciation.

4. Two –Way Interaction: It is a two way interaction that may take place in various ways like

- In case of one - to - one interviews: Generally it occurs between a candidate and a single interviewer. These are generally structured and the candidates are generally asked the common questions.

- In case of panel interviews: These are conducted between the interviewee and more than a single interviewer. Each member of the committee may focus on particular aspects of evaluation to ensure effective decision making.

5. Informality: The success of any job interview mainly depends on the informal and friendly atmosphere where in the candidates get opportunities to give their best. So, an interview will not achieve its goals if the tension is not reduced by developing a friendly relation between the interviewee and the interviewers.

9.4: Job Interview Types

Different types of interviews are held for different fields and positions. Some of them are discussed below:

1. Telephonic Interview

This is a common form of interview and is specially conducted when the interviewees do not reside near the prospective employer or during a critical situation like COVID'2019. It is been used as a tool for the first round of screening in case of large number of applicants. The most advantage of this process is cost effectiveness.

2. Technical Interview

This is an essential round of screening. In this process of interview the experts of the panel try to evaluate the technical acquaintance of the interviewee. The interviewer used to ask the questions based on the fundamental concepts of the candidate's domain knowledge, applications and the skill to relate the knowledge in other related fields. Look at the sample of a technical question

Questions: How does airplane fly?

Answer: Sir, in the flying of an aeroplane, the theory of Bernolli is applicable where by virtue of the drag and lift force it goes in the air

3. Behavioural Interview

It has been considered as a common type of "job interview" in the modern workplace. It is based on the view that a candidate's past behaviour is considered as the best indicator of his/ her future performance. In behavioural interview, the selection board generally asks the interviewee to remember specific instances they have faced and try to assess their reaction on it. The mode of questions generally asked in a Behavioural interview is as follows:

Questions: We are interested to know a project where you took a lead. What was your action plan?

Questions: Can you mention a project you worked on where the requirements changed midstream. What did you do?

4. Psychometric Test

To judge the personality of a candidate, sometimes, these tests are administered. Presently the test is becoming a part and parcel of a selection procedure in job interview process. In this test, almost fifty to sixty questions are asked to evaluate aptitude and knowledge of the applicant. After clearing the round, he/she is asked to attend a GD (Group discussion) round and finally HR (Human Resource) round.

5. Stress Interview

In stress interview the applicant is asked a number of questions rapidly to assess his/her capability to handle the stressed situations. The candidates are required to be mentally alert since they are asked multiple questions at a time. You should stay calm during such sessions. The main aim of this interviewing process is to test an applicant's behaviour in a hectic situation. Stress interviews may include excessive workload, dealing with more than one project at a time. Given below are some sample questions of a stress interview:

1st Questions: You have shared your opinion with us that during COVID, 2019 the market, shopping mall should be closed totally till the vaccine is invented. It would stop the rapid fast transfer of virus among the people.

Immediately the 2nd Question may be asked

2nd Question: Now tell us how it will effect on the business transitions and ultimately influence the economy of India?

9.5: Pre Interview Preparation Techniques

A 'job interview' is a formal, structured and systematic interaction between the applicant and the interview board members. The candidate need to set up a relationship, impress the interviewers and convince them that he/she is fit for the job.

Preparing well is the key success for an interview. Facing a 'job interview' whether a personal interview, a telephonic interview or through videoconferencing –it needs to prepare it systematically. Pre-interview preparation techniques include self-analysis, skill assessment, company analysis, job analysis, subject revision and developing the interview file.

1. Self-analysis

We cannot project ourselves successfully unless we know our strong and weak point properly. Self-analysis is required for effective planning for a job applicant. It includes analyzing our background; identify our major accomplishments, achievements, special interest and hobbies and career goals

i) Analyzing our Background

We should begin self-analysis with a critical analysis of our educational and professional background. It is relevant to search out the answer of the question: Do we have the proper background for the job? The candidate may have impressive credentials and experience. Usually the interviewers are interested to know the background of the applicant. A few frequently asked questions are given below:

"We would like to know about you."

"Describe yourself in a few sentences"

ii) Identify our Major Accomplishments:

An accomplishment can be defined as 'completion of a specific task by means of one's skill. A candidate should identify and make the list of such accomplishments. Anything you did during school life that showed positive dimensions of your personality. Next you may explore your college life to identify instances that you did well. Bearing the professional experience, you should identify situational problem that you could handle effectively. Some questions that may be asked you to reflect on your accomplishment include:

"Have you ever solved a problem?"

"Tell us about a situational problem you faced and solved."

iii) Achievements

Achievement shows our educational and professional success and distinguishes a successful person from the non-achievers. You should make a particular list of scholarship, fellowships, awards, prizes, distinctions, certificates or anything that shows achievement or recognition. The interviewers may ask the straight questions like:

"What are your achievements?"

"Have you ever done anything that has given you a sense of achievements?"

iv) Special Interest and Hobbies

The third aspect of self-analysis is identifying special interest and hobbies. Such activities may be listed. As your Curriculum Vitae (CV) may also include your hobbies, interest and activities, you need to prepare yourself to justify them during an interview. As most organizations prefer dynamic and active employees, special interests and activities must show the candidate as a dynamic and energetic person who can accept all kind of challenges.

v) Career Goals

A candidate must analyze your career goals- your ambition in life, your career objectives. So, it is essential to analyze your career objectives. you have applied for. Some frequently asked questions related to career goals which are mentioned below:

"Mention your career goals?"

"We would like to know your career objectives."

2. Skill Assessment

Skill assessment is a systematic process of analyzing your skill. Every job usually has a set of functions that requires certain skills to perform. The main function of a interview for a job is to evaluate the skill of the job seeker to carry out the functions associated with the assigned job. Thus analyzing skill is a vital part of preparation of an interview. To assess this, a systematic approach should be adopted. First of all you need to prepare a list of your skills. After that examine how many of your skills match with the required job. Most employers used to see the match between the candidate's skills and the requirements for the job. They may ask the following questions:

"How will you rate yourself for the post on a scale of one to ten?"

"What are your strengths?"

2. Company Analysis

Researching an organization involves gathering information of the organization like its nature of business, areas of operations, products or services, hierarchical structure, financial condition, corporate culture, growth rate etc. There are many ways to research the organization. It is obvious to visit the website of the company. In addition you can visit the library to look for relevant information of any organization. You may refer to company directories, company reports and other business journals. Also you can go through the company's brochures and recent annual report. Finally, you may get the feedback by talking to the person working in that organization. Interviews may ask a few questions to check your awareness about the organization. The questions may include:

"What do you know about this company?"

"How do you rate this company?"

3. Job Analysis

You should have the knowledge about the position so that you can respond to the questions asked to test your suitability for the post. Moreover, without sufficient knowledge for the position you are not in a position to give answers the following questions:

"Why you interested to take this job?"

"What are the channels of career enhancement?"

"What are the responsibilities related with this job?"

4. Subject Revision

An interview for a job is being arranged to assess the candidate's level of knowledge and technical expertise. Most of the organizations stress on evaluating the subject competence of candidates. Subject basics must be clear because the experts of selection board might test your commend on your subject. It is therefore advisable to revise one's subject knowledge before appearing the interview.

5. Developing the Interview File

An interview preparation demands a professional approach. Therefore you should develop an interview file that may contain the following paper and documents:

- Interview letter
- Original degrees, testimonials (Keep ready of all self-attested copies)
- Experience Certificate

- Certificate of Merit
- Copies of Your Resume
- Your Visiting Card
- Other relevant papers that might be needed during interview.

An index of all papers and documents in the file makes for easy reference and location. Keeping everything ready in order will help out in projecting yourself as an organized person.

9.6: Employer's Expectations from an Interview

We may classify the information which an employer seek while considering a candidate suitable for a post. These may be classified into the following subheadings:

i) State of Health: Every organization expects the employees should be in healthy state. A healthy state of employee can only put the optimum output for the organization. Moreover a company requires thorough medical examinations for a new entrant.

ii) Attainments: A probe is made to verify what is written by the candidate in the CV and to assess the nature and quality of his achievements

iii) Aptitude: Certain questions are directed merely to assess the candidate's aptitude for the position he/she has applied.

iv) Confidence: An observation is being made for the response of the interviewee to evaluate the extent of his/her grasp and level of confidence.

v) Field of Interest: An attempt is made to understand the other dimension of the candidate's personality by encouraging him/her to speak about his/her intellectual or social pursuits.

vi) Disposition: Essential information that all employers would seek from a applicant is the capability to work with others.

9.7: Answering Strategies

The way a question is answered reflects a person's communication ability. The following seven factors will surely help in improving the quality of answers during an interview processes are attentiveness, accuracy, brevity, focus, clarity, positive attitude and logical thinking. These are discussed briefly discussed below:

i) Attentiveness

When a person attends an interview for a job, he/she cannot answer the interview's question correctly unless he/ she is listening properly. So it is recommended that interviewee should listen to the interviewer attentively to understand the question and then respond to it.

ii) Accuracy

It is recommended for a job seeker to give special attention to dates, timelines, persons, places and other relevant details. Giving an incorrect or incomplete answer may be a factor for rejection in the interview.

iii) Brevity

The interviewee should be brief and to the point while answering the questions. He/ she listen carefully and answer only what is asked. A long answer does not essentially mean a better answer, it is usually otherwise.

iv) Focus

The applicant should be focused and specific. The more specific the answer, the more convinced the interviewers as a suitable candidate for the position. Concrete and specific words and phrases should be used and obscure and vague words that may confuse the interviewers should be avoided.

v) Clarity

It is expected that a candidate should answer directly and clearly. Clearness of expression generally reflects clarity of thought and professionalism of a candidate.

vi) Positive Attitude

The reply made by a candidate should reflect his/her positive attitude. It is vital for an interviewee to be positive and answer even negative or sensitive questions in a positive way.

vii) Logical Thinking

The skill to think logically is always impressive during an interview. A reply to the interviewers should always be rational and logical.

9.8: Review of General Interview Questions

There are some frequently asked questions usually asked in an interview, which are given here. Practicing replies to these questions and rehearsing will definitely develop confidence of the candidate and will help in improving job interviewing skills.

We would like to know about you.

Hints to the answer: *You need to have a brief description highlighting one's back ground, education, skills, and experience may be given.*

We are Interested to Know your Academic Achievements:

Hints to the answer: *You should give a direct answer mentioning your achievements. You need to enlist your academic ability and excellence.*

Tell about your Work Experience

Hints to the answer: *This is a straight question asking you to describe your experiences.* The answer should be brief and specific

Mention your career objectives? / What type of position you are looking for?

Hints to the answer: *A positive answer to this question would include a focused statement expressing the career goals in relation to the targeted position.*

Why you are Considering Yourself that you are fit for this Position?

Hints to the answer: *The interviewers want to know your self assessment about the suitability for the pos. You should be able to establish how well your knowledge, qualifications, skills match with the job*

Why you are Interested to Join our Company?

Hints to the answer: *Interviewers would like to test your knowledge about their organization and your interest to work with them. This question should be answered in the light of the company analysis*

Mention your Strength?

Hints to the answer: *Interviewer would like to know if your strength matches the need of the job. This is opportunity to highlight your strength. Some of the qualities you can mention are persistence, dedication, commitment, leadership, team building skills, organizational skills etc.*

What is your Weakness?

Hints to the answer: *Be careful while answering the question. To stand out, be more original and state a weakness, and then emphasize what you have done to overcome it*

Do you Consider Yourself as a Team player?

Hints to the answer: *You are of course a 'team player'. You should ready with examples which shows that you perform better in a team rather than for yourself.*

Where do you see Yourself Five Years Down the Line?

Hints to the answer: *This is a chance for you to demonstrate your long –term planning capacities. They are asking for your career aspirations. Tell them that you want to see yourself in a role where you will handle more responsibilities effectively and capably.*

May we Consider you as an Asset to this Organization?

Hints to the answer: *You should be keenly looking for this question. It gives you a opportunity to highlight your strong area.*

How do you Define Success?

Hints to the answer: *You have to answer it with full of your confidence. This may answer like "Sir the definition of success may differ from person to person. In my opinion "success is the status of having achieved and accomplished an aim or objective."*

9.9: Summary:

Concept and Meaning of Job Interviews: It provides the best opportunity to examine the relevance of an applicant's knowledge skill and experience. It is also a fact that job interview is an effective technique used for evaluating the fitness of a candidate for a position. It could be either face to face meeting or formal conversation over phone or videoconferencing between a candidate and the interviewer/(s) or the placement agencies work for the concerned employers. In the modern technological advanced world job interviews are more challenging

Process of Job Interviews: Three steps process which includes: gather information, establishing a rapport and finally closing of interview

Characteristics of Job Interviews: It is prearranged and planed conversation characterized by a defined purpose and some level of informality. There are five aspects involved in this process like planning. Purpose, conversation, two way interaction and informality.

Types of Job Interviews: Different types of interviews for different fields and positions like: Telephonic Interview, Technical Interview, Behavioral Interview, Psychometric test, Stress Interview.

Pre Interview Preparation Techniques: Facing an interview whether a face to face personal interview, a telephonic interview or through videoconferencing –is easier when one prepare for it systematically. Pre-interview preparation techniques include self-analysis, skill assessment, company analysis, job analysis, subject revision and developing the interview file.

Employer's Expectations from a Job Interview: An employer seek while considering a person is fit for a job are mainly the following parameters

- **State of Health:** Every organization expects its people to be in healthy state.
- **Attainments:** A probe is made through searching questions to verify what is written by the candidate in the CV and to assess the nature and quality of his achievements
- **Aptitude:** Certain questions are directed merely to find out the candidate's aptitude for the job
- **Confidence:** A close observation is made based on the response of the interviewee to evaluate the extent of his/her level of confidence.
- **Field of Interest:** An attempt to make to understand the other dimension of the personality of the job aspirant.
- **Disposition:** Essential information that all employers would like to have is whether the candidate has the ability to work with others.

Answering Strategies: The way a question is answered reflects a person's communication ability. The following seven factors which help in improving the quality of answers are attentiveness, accuracy, brevity, focus, clarity, positive attitude and logical thinking.

9.10: Glossary

Aptitude: Certain questions are directed to evaluate the candidate's aptitude for the job

Attainments: A probe is made through searching questions to verify what is written by the candidate in the CV and to assess the nature and quality of his achievements

Accomplishments: An accomplishment can be explained as the completion of a particular job with the help of one's skill. A candidate should identify and make a list of such accomplishments.

Behavioural Interview: This is a common type of interview in the modern workplace. It is based on the candidate's past behaviour which is considered as the best indicator of his/ her future performance.

Company Analysis: Researching an organization involves gathering information about the company in terms of its nature of business, areas of operations, products or services, hierarchical structure, financial condition, corporate culture, growth rate etc.

Conversation: It is basically a conversation between the recruiters and the job applicant where mainly question – answer session is been occurred

Career Goals: A candidate must analyze his /her career objectives and goals before appearing for an interview

Closing Interview: The interviewee needs to be well prepared for the closing of interview with his / her closing remarks

Disposition: Most of the employers would like to know the capacity of the candidate to work with others.

Establishing a Rapport: To create a quick rapport with the selection board members.

Informality: The success of any job interview mainly depends on the informal and friendly atmosphere where in the candidates get opportunities to give their best.

Job Analysis: It is the process of assembling and analyzing information about the job.

Job Interviews: It provides the best opportunity to examine the relevance of an applicant's knowledge, skill and experience fit for the job.

Psychometric Test: To judge a candidate personality, very often, psychometric tests are administered.

Skill Assessment: Skill assessment is the unique process of analyzing the skills of a candidate appearing for a job interview.

Stress Interview: The candidate is asked a series of questions rapidly to assess his/her capability to handle the stressed situations

Telephonic Interview: This is a common form of interview process. This is specially conducted when the candidate does not reside near the prospective employer.

Technical Interview: This is an essential round of screening. In this process of interview, the experts of the panel try to find out the technical knowledge of the interviewee.

9.11: Self-Assessment Questions

1. What is a job interview? Discuss the process of a job interview in detail.
2. Mention the main characteristics of Job Interviews
3. 'There are various types of job interviews that are held for different fields and positions'- Mention the main types of job interviews
4. Mention the pre interview preparation techniques that should be adopted by a candidate for appearing in a job interview.
5. Discuss the various qualities of a candidate that are evaluated during an interview.
6. Mention the employer's expectations from a interviewee
7. Describe the main factors which help in improving the quality of answers during an interview
8. Write short notes on:

   i) Psychometric Test

   ii) Stress Interview
   iii) Telephonic Interview
   iv) Technical Interview
   v) Self-analysis
   vi) Company Analysis

9. Your placements will be commenced in the next month. What preparations will you make for the interview?

10. How do you prove your skills and traits by providing examples from your experience with regard to the following parameters:
    a) Communication Skills
    b) Confidence
    c) Positive Attitude
    d) Interpersonal Skills
    e) Integrity

Chapter-10

Applications of Electronic Tools in Business Communication

Contents

10.0: Learning Objectives

You will understand

- Technical Communication: concept and its importance.

- We have mentioned the technological changes and their effects on business communication
- Types of technology based communication have discussed with examples
- We have discussed the electronic tools applied in business communication
- Guidelines for writing E mails have given with practical examples.
- We have provided the "Glossary"
- Conceptual questions are given which is extremely helpful for the students

10.1: Technical Based Communication

Presently we are in an age of 'Information Technology'. 'Communication is considered as a key success to any business organization'! We are in use of different kinds of communication through information technology based tools. Technology is impacting the way people learn and apply" business communication skills" in their workplace.

Presently people need to learn the methods necessary to communicate effectively, efficiently and professionally. Mobile has reformed the ways we used to enhance our daily lives in many ways. The most modern telephone is cellular phone, or commonly called a "cell phone". It is intended to give the user maximum freedom to move with a phone. Uses of cellular phone are rapidly increasing in accordance with its utility. Access in Mobile internet is a global phenomenon with even great implications.

10.2: Importance of Technical Based Communication

As technology moved front and centre in many business, it has stopped being a 'support function' and has now become the prime factor to get the work done. Technology plays a strong role in preserving, or undermining, trust in business connections

In a business environment, it is important to learn to secure information in phone number, statistics, or research report. It also helps to learn how to use various forms of technology for communicating more easily, more effectively and efficiently.

Today, information is a mass product and obviously not a scarce resource. Our need for information is insatiable and inexorable.

'Internet' facilitates worldwide interconnections of computers sitting in university labs or business houses. The capability to access the information stored in thousands of computers worldwide to chat with anyone around the globe at round the clock bestows incredible power to anyone who knows to retrieve, evaluate and share that information.

10.3: Technology and Business Communication

It is difficult to deny that there are huge effects of technology on businesses. Regardless of the size, scope of the company, the launch of internet has made its mark.

The way of communication is constantly developing, in alignment of the technological advancement. Technology has made significant, permanent changes to how businesses communicate. We can mention the different ways of business communication which are changed due to latest technological advancement.

i) Immediacy

By increasing immediacy, technological changes marked the business environment. "Real-Time Technology" is a special type of technological progress which typifies the contemporary communication in business. Presently the employees need not depend on phone for sending a lengthy email to connect with their colleagues as the "IM" conversation can reduces the delay in action that often results from an email conversation. The workers, working in remote are now able to work with teammates through these applications.

ii) Security

The prime requirements of a business is to ensure secured communication. It is justified, due to extensive use of email in workplace. The "Digital Communication" is now most secured and multidimensional.

iii) Automation

The modern business communication dynamic changes have come through automation. With the help of automation, the companies can utilize their resources to increase efficiency in the business. In this context we may put the reference of other latest technology "Voice over Internet Protocol" (VoIP). This technology automatically places and receives calls, permitting the employees to focus their time elsewhere.

iv) Versatility

Versatility plays a significant role in technological upliftment in business. Without making contact or speak with the co-workers, employees can use the technology by means of presentations. Presentations are now much more interactive, easy to follow and keep the audience engaged and comprehends the content.

Externally, technology helps to communicate better with the customers or interested consumers by better understanding their wants and needs. Technology like "Artificial Intelligence" builds an understanding with the customers.

Contemporary communication in a business is unique because it does not through a singular path. A few years back business communications were limited to tools like phone calls, email, fax, presently communication is more conversational than ever.

10.4: Types of Technology based Communication

Mobile communication is now an essential part of business. People require the capacity to communicate while they move around within the organization and the outside world. There are various forms in communication process, which are mainly based on modern technology. They may be grouped as:

i) Computer

ii) Model Letters Database

iii) Copier

iv) Cell phones or Mobiles

v) FAX machine

Let us discuss briefly each of them

i) Computer

Knowledge of the electronic technology is significant to your understanding of the communication in business. In recent years, computer software has developed that checks writing for corrections along with for certain principles of styles. You can easily write a rough draft of a document using the function of "word processing". From these programmes, you also receive analyses of your work with suggestions for betterment. Spelling checkers is also very useful programs. More recent spelling checkers, however, are an important part of "Word Processing" program. Even each word of the document is being tested against the dictionary. If a word spelling that doesn't match with the dictionary is flagged on the screen. Some spelling checkers even suggest alternative spellings.

ii) Model Letters Database

"Floppy disk" comprising model letters are available in computers. These databases of business letters cover common situations for corresponding credit responses, sales, collections, customer relations and so on. Undoubtedly such letters can save time. Moreover such letters are unlikely to reflect the personality, which is a prime requirement of a good letter. Hence it is suggested to develop your own model letters, put them on disks, and adopt them to specific situations.

iii) Copiers

In most offices today, copiers are used to replicate of an original document instantly. Some modern copier machines are small and handy. The larger ones are immobile but may reduce or expand original pages, editable, duplicate both sides automatically and produce multiple copies with great speed. In addition, some copies can duplicate colors. Without questions, copiers are essential in a modern electronic office.

iv) Cell Phone / Mobiles

It provides the fastest feedback and proves to be very effective in communication especially with the employees engaged in staff functions. These are much more effective at ensuring direct contact with the individual. Despite short term problems like signal strength, get connected from remote location, high charges when roaming etc. the mobile phones are influencing the business communication. Cell phones allow instantaneous communication with improved quality and quantity of information.

In cell phone, voice technologies like 'voice processing' and 'voice synthesizing' have direct influence on communication. 'Voice Processing', is the recording devices to answer telephone calls. Recording machines can receive and send to incoming callers. A 'Remote Beeper' is used to determine when a call was received, and who called. It is even possible to recognize the place and phone number from which a call originated. 'Voice synthesizing' means accessing stored written materials and having it read over the telephone with prerecorded words.

v) FAX Machine

It scans a document, converts the 'information' into 'electronic impulses' and send these to a facsimile receiver. The receiver immediately converts these impulses into a graphic form. The facsimile is not limited to the printed word; it can transmit pictures, charts etc. It is fast and relatively cost effective tool.

10.5: Applications of Electronic Tools in Business Communication

1. E- Mail

Electronic mail called as "E-mail" came into existence in twentieth century. This progeny of technology took over from all other methods to exchange the information and now it is almost impossible to conceive of a world where persons do not share their views, ideas and information through e mails. Following are a few factors which have made email writings such a phenomenon in our times:

- **E-mails are very Fast and Easy to Operate:** One reason why emails are preferred is they are easy, prompt, and fast to use. Once you compose a mail, it can send to many people as required, instantaneously. Practically, in an "email" message, you can attach large files containing of data, spreadsheets, voluminous reports, lengthy procedures, elaborate schedules, details proposals etc that you desire to send to anybody across the world.
- **E-mails offer Flexibility in Tone and Style:** Now-a-days, we are habituated to apply short cuts in all that we write and speak. Since no traditional way of communication offers this flexibility, electronic mail is lapped up most readily by us. Aided by the speed generated through the medium of expression, we can able to carve messages which are easy to compose and quick to send. Moreover, since emails are used not just professionally but also personality, a sense of informality starts creeping into our style as soon as we set ourselves into composing an email.
- **E-mails Capture the Essence of Age:** Advancement in technology have added frantic pace to our lives. In this fast-paced life, anything that saves time for us is certainly most welcome and becomes most desirable.
- **E-mails become Legal and Valid:** Though started informally, emails are now regarded as a "valid" and "tenable proof" to someone's claims legally. The change of medium thus does not take away the essentials presence of the receiver and the sender in the process of communication

2. Teleconferencing

It means telephonic conversation with two or more person. Here the "communication network technology" is being used to connect participant's voice.

The various types of "Teleconferencing" are mentioned below:

A) Audio Conference

B) Audio Graphic Conference

C) Video Conference

D) Computer Conference

Let us discuss in short for each of them

A) Audio Conference: It involves transmission of voice only which are amplified by the speaker system. It can usually handle over telephone line and is cost effective communication system. Presently all most all meetings are been conducted through the audio conference.

B) Audio Graphic Conference: It offers both- voice and graphic display. The most commonly used graphic complement is a "facsimile machine".

C) Video Conference: It has emerged as a form of teleconferencing and is considered as a new, fast growing medium. It combines of both audio and video to offer voice communication and image The three basic systems are there named: "Freeze Frame", "Compressed" and "Full Motion Video". It is potential as it saves travel cost and time. "Video Conferencing" are of two types :

i) Point to Point Conferencing: Its communication link between any two sites.

ii) Multipoint Conferencing: It acts as a link between different of locations where the Participants from different sites can hear to each other. The advantages of this video conferencing are as follows:

- Increase Productivity
- Increase Quality of Work

- Time and money saver
- Build Relationships
- Improves Communication

D) Computer Conference: It is conducted through telephone lines through the help of computers and modems. By using electronic mail, one can send the reports, updates and newsletter to anyone. There are two kinds of computer conferencing:

i) **Delayed Time:** The conference is taking place in a simple shared "mail box"

ii) **Real Time:** It is interactive and more closely resemble telephone conferencing call. There are some major benefits of teleconferencing which are explained below

i) **More Information –Not people:** Electronic transmit is more effective rather than physically reach to a site.

ii) **Save Time:** One or many sources is received in many places instantly. Due to smooth Communication, the meetings are conducted more effectively.

iii) **Lower Cost:** It reduces travelling costs by keeping employees in the office, speeding up production development cycles.

iv) **Accessible**: It reaches through any organization site in the world.

v) **Larger Audiences:** More people can attend. The larger the audience, the lower -cost per individual.

vi) **Adoptable:** Useful for business, association, hospitals and institutions to discuss, educate, train

viii) **Flexible:** A transmit or receive site can be located anywhere.

ix) **Security:** Signals can be translated as per requirement.

3. Image Scanning

An image scanner allows to convert photos and diagrams into electronic files swiftly. People can get the advantage to scan and send the files immediately through internet. For example, an architectural firm can scan a plan, transmits it to the client, receives changes and makes necessary modifications.

4. Radio Frequency Identification (RFID)

This technology uses "Radio Frequency Waves" to transfer data. RFID technology is used in many places like shopping malls, libraries etc. at a rapid pace.

5. SMS:

"SMS" is the abbreviation of "Short Message Service". SMS is used in social and business applications such as: stock quotations, electronic voting or e- mail notification. It supports to send and receive of text, images, animation and sound.

The main benefits of SMS are given below:

- Notifications on delivery with alerts
- Reliable message delivery
- Enable the wireless data access for corporate user
- Notification mechanisms for newer services for those using "Wireless Applications Protocols"
- Integration with other data and internet based applications.

6. Multimedia Messaging Service (MMS)

Multimedia Messaging is just around the corner and is likely a popular messaging service in future. It is a new and prominent wireless standard for multimedia.

10.6: Principles for Writing E-mails

Emails are the pieces of communication. Due to absence of a settled convention, it becomes a challenge to compose a mail that is proper in all respects. By following a few principles, we can cast our email in effective manner:

i) Use Subject Lines Effectively: While composing an email, we do not give any importance to "subject line" at all. It is essential to think subject before shooting it off from the email box. It suggests what little worth we assign to choose an appropriate "subject line" to our message. Observed seriously, however, we realize the "subject line" is as important as the message itself.. In fact in today's world, when people are swarmed with endless growing mails in their mailbox, a catchy subject line can distinguish a meaningful mail from many other trash mails.

The following "subject lines" extracted from professional emails. See how the revised "subject lines" add to the worth of a message:

Original subject line of a message	Revised subject line
Meeting	Schedule of Meeting
Re: Delay	Re: Delay in consignment Delivery
Retail outlet	Announcement regarding Retail outlet
Absent	Overcoming Absenteeism
Just like that	Exchanging Pleasantries

ii) Start Writing Courteously: Regarding e mails there is a misconception that these are informal pieces of interaction and hence courtesy is not much desired. While writing an email, keep in mind that though a degree of informality is essentially part and parcel of such communication, disregarding courtesy and politeness is not desirable. It may be explained with the help of the following examples:

Original message	Modified version
Madam, Have you received any communication from our office? If yes, please kick the mail back. Please arrange to send the status. Thanks PC	Dear Madam, Kindly share the information regarding the schedule for the talk by the Marketing personnel. Being from the similar field, I am keenly interested to listen from you. Thanks & Regards Partha Chatterjee GM -Marketing ABC Co Ltd

iii) A Proper Beginning: The style of an e-mail should not essentially differ much from that of a business letter. This is not required to start in a manner that seems abrupt, unofficial, and jerky. Take a look, for instance, at revised beginning of an e-mail with the tone and tenor that it needs to display:

Initial message	Modified version
Dear Mr Chairperson, I am unable to attend the Board Meeting, as I shall be out of station.	Dear Mr Chairperson, Thank you for informing me about the Board Meeting scheduled in the next week. However due to some other pressing urgent matters, I need to move to Delhi. Nevertheless, I would be available on-line.

iv) Avoid Crippled Spelling: A big number of e-mails are written similarly like a message on a mobile. Writing email shorthand can give a serious professional embarrassment. Writing thus can lose one's credibility.

10.7: Summary

Technical Based Communication

Communication plays a vital role to any business success. We use information technology based tools, which provide us multiple ways for exchanging information. Technology is impacting the way people learn and apply skills in business communication in their workplace.

"Cell phone" is being planned to give the user maximum freedom of moving while using a telephone. The usage of cellular phone is rapidly increasing in accordance with its utility. Internet access through mobile is a global phenomenon with even great implications.

Importance of Technical Based Communication

As technology moved front and centre in many business, it has stopped being a 'support function'. Technology plays a strong role in preserving, or undermining, trust in business relations. In a business environment, it is vital to learn how to secure the information.

Today, information is a mass product and not a scarce resource. The most useful tool in this connection is the 'Internet' which facilitates worldwide interconnections of computers sitting in university labs or business houses. The facility to access the information stored in thousands of computers worldwide to chat with anyone around the globe bestows incredible power to anyone who possess the knowledge to retrieve, evaluate and share that information.

Technological Advancement and Business Communication

Presently the technological progression put a major effects on business. Regardless of the size, scope of the company, the initiation of internet, mobile devices and "artificial intelligence" has made its mark.Technology has made significant, permanent changes to how businesses communicate. There are a few ways that business communication has transformed due to technology. For examples:

Immediacy: Technology has changed the business environment through immediacy

Security: To ensure and confirm secured communication is the primary requirements to any business organization

Automation: The modern business communication is mainly depends on automation. Due to technological development, the communication becomes easier.

Versatility: It is a helpful in technological improvement in modern business scenario.

Types of Technology based Communication

There are various methods in communication process, which are mainly based on modern technology.

- **Computer**: Presently the software has developed that checks writing for corrections and for certain principles of styles. By using "word processing" function, anyone can write a rough draft of a document. From these programmes, you also receive analyses of your work with suggestions for betterment. Spelling checkers is also very useful programs.
- **Model Letters Database:** These databases of business letters cover common situations for corresponding credit responses, sales, collections, customer relations and so on.
- **Copiers:** In most offices today, copiers are being used to replicate of an original document instantly. Some modern copier machines are small and handy. The larger ones are immobile but may reduce or expand original pages, editable, duplicate both sides automatically and produce multiple copies with great speed.
- **Mobiles:** It provides the fastest feedback and proves to be very effective in communication especially with the employees engaged in staff functions. Cell phones are much more effective at ensuring direct contact with the individual

rather than the mere transmission of a message to his /her desk.

- **FAX Machine:** It scans a document, converts the information into 'electronic impulses' and send to a facsimile receiver.
- **Applications of Electronic Tools in Business Communication:** The following tools are generally applied for business communication
- **E- mail:** Electronic mail came into existence in twentieth century. With the help of this technology views, ideas .information and data can be shared.
- **Teleconferencing:** It means meeting over phone with two or more participants .There are various types of teleconferencing like Audio Conference, Audio Graphic Conference, Video Conference and Computer Conference
- **Image Scanning:** It allows workers to convert diagrams and photos into electronic files for transmission.
- **RFID:** This is an abbreviated form of Radio Frequency Identification.
- **SMS:** SMS is a universal communication tool and can be delivered to any mobile phone. There are some benefits of using SMS like notifications on delivery, reliable and guaranteed message delivery, increased productivity of the subscriber etc.
- **MMS: It stands for "Multimedia Messaging Service".** This is considered as a new and prominent wireless standard for multimedia.
- **Video Conferencing:** This is a combination of audio and video. Video conferencing are of two types "Point to Point Conferencing" and Multipoint Conferencing.

10.8: Glossary

- **Cell Phone:** A communication tool which provides the fastest feedback and proves to be very effective in communication
- **Copiers:** A machine which reproduces mass duplications of an original document instantly
- **E- Mail:** Through E –Mail one can share his/her views, ideas or information
- **FAX machine:** The machine can scan a document, converts into electronic impulses and send to a facsimile receiver. It is fast and relatively cost effective tool.
- **Image Scanner:** It allows to convert diagrams, photos, etc. into electronic files for the purpose of storage as well as transmission.
- **Internet:** It facilitates worldwide interconnections of computers
- **MMS:** It stands for "Multimedia Messaging Service" It is an accepted messaging service in the field of communication. Also considered as a latest and prominent wireless standard for multimedia.
- **RFID: "Radio Frequency Identification"** are chips that respond to "radio waves" with encoded information, allowing companies to tag and track items and materials.
- **SMS:** Full form **is "Short Message Services"** and broadly used features on mobile phone and is considered as a trusted communication tool.
- **Teleconferencing:** This is live "real time session" among multiple participants and can listen and see to each other with the facility of sharing data.

10.9:Self-Assessment Questions

1. What is Technology –based communication and why is it important in today's business world?
2. Name and discuss the different tools to access electronic information?
3. State the various tools available to share electronic information?
4. Mention different mobile communication tools?
5. "IT plays a vital function in communication process" – Justify the statement.
6. How the technological changes effects on business communication?
7. "Video Conferencing helps to disrupt barriers of distance among businesses." Elaborate the statement.
8. State the advantages of SMS in "Electronic Business Communications"?
9. What is "Teleconferencing"? What are the benefits of Teleconferencing?
10. Write short notes on:
    a) RFID
    b) MMS
    c) Copiers
    d) FAX machine
11. Discuss the main features of an e-mail. Highlight writing techniques required to draft effective professional emails.

Glossary

Accomplishments: An accomplishment can be explained as the completion of a particular job with the help of one's skill. A candidate should identify and make a list of such accomplishments.

Abstract: The abstract is the most important elements of a technical article. The abstract of a paper captures the essence of the research. It summarizes the essential information in the article focusing on key facts, findings, observations, results, conclusions, and recommendations.

Analytical Report: An analytical report is not only contains the facts, views and opinions of reporters and others but also includes the causes for an issue or an event and required remedial action with recommendations.

Appendix: Statistical data, charts, and diagrams that are not generally included in the main body of the report are mentioned here.

Audio Visual Aids: It refers to the equipment available to us for amplifying our message.

Auto Content Wizard: It is a tool that would guide you through the process of customizing a predesigned document.

Behavioural Interview: This is a common type of interview in the modern workplace. It is based on the candidate's past behaviour which is considered as the best indicator of his/ her future performance.

Bibliography: This is a list of books and journals which are taken into consideration prior to or during the preparation of a report.

Blogs: It is place where you can write your opinion or you can discuss any particular topic of your interest.

Body Language: It is the posture of the body. Signs of body language are folded hands, lack of eye contact, slouched back, straight face, and not paying attention.

Career Goals: A candidate must analyze his /her career objectives and goals before appearing for an interview

Casual Pattern: In this pattern the ideas are divided into two major components-causes and their effects.

Cell Phone: A communication tool which provides the fastest feedback and proves to be very effective in communication

Chronological Pattern: Chronological Pattern is the most commonly used pattern for organizing a speech.

Circular: Office circular is formal in nature is meant to bring the notice of a certain audience matters of importance to the organization.

Closing Interview: The interviewee needs to be well prepared for the closing of interview with his / her closing remarks

Company Analysis: Researching an organization involves gathering information about the company in terms of its nature of business, areas of operations, products or services, hierarchical structure, financial condition, corporate culture, growth rate etc.

Conference Paper: It is the text of a paper that the author has presented in a seminar, conference or workshop.

Copiers: A machine which reproduces mass duplications of an original document instantly

Curriculum Vitae: Curriculum Vitae reflection of the candidate's personality. There is no specific design for resume.

The design of a resume largely depends on a person's back round, employment needs, career goals and professional conventions in the area of specialization.

Diagonal Communication: It is also termed as "Spiral Communication". Sometimes communication flows between persons of different levels of hierarchy and have no direct reporting authority. 'Diagonal Communication' flows in all directions as it has no rigid norms of communication protocol.

Dialog Box: It enables you to choose essential features of a basic presentation.

Downward Communication: When a communication comes from higher level to the lower level of employees, it called as Downward Communication.

E- Mail: Through E –Mail one can share his/her views, ideas or information

Executive Summary: It is often circulated to the concerned authority for taking a decision. A well written, comprehensive, and concise summary would be convincing for accepting the project.

Extra Personal Communication: The communication with non-human entities such as animals, birds etc. is termed as extra personal communication.

Facial Expression: It is basically the expression of a face of by which a person can express his joy, sorrow, fear, anger, etc.

Factual Topics: In a formal GD, the participants are given topics which are factual in nature.

FAX Machine: The machine can scan a document, converts into electronic impulses and send to a facsimile receiver. It is fast and relatively cost effective tool.

Filmstrip and Slide Projector: Filmstrips are a sequence of transparencies on 8 or 16 mm films.

Flicker: It is an image and video hosting platform for online community. Photos can be shared in this platform.

Formal Report: Formal reports are prepared as per the formal structure and established rules and presented before the appropriate authority.

Glossary: A glossary is a list of some technical or special words with their explanations.

Group Discussion (GD): This is a methodical 'oral exchange of information', thought and opinion about a specific topic, issue and problem.

Horizontal Communication: It occurs between peer group or the people working on the same level of an organization.

Image Scanner: It allows to convert diagrams, photos, etc. into electronic files for the purpose of storage as well as transmission.

Improper Encoding: Improper barrier is a frequent barrier in the process of communication.

Index: This is an alphabetical list of subjects of the report. An index assists the reader to trace any topic simply and quickly.

Informal Report: Informal report is prepared as per the ease of the reporter and presented before the person as per the requirement.

Informational Report: The Informational reports only present the facts and summary without analysing, interpreting, and making recommendations.

Instagram: It is a Platform through which photograph and video may be shared freely in different social networking sites. You can also give special effects to your photographs and videos through this platform.

Instant Messaging: Instant messaging is one kind of online conversation that allows you to send and receive concise written messages in real time.

Internet: It facilitates worldwide interconnections of computers

Intrapersonal Communication: Whenever communication takes places within an individual, it is called 'Intrapersonal Communication'.

Job Analysis: It is the process of assembling and analysing information about the job.

Journal Article: A journal article is the communication of technical information in a structured form as per the format given by the publishing authority.

Job Interviews: It provides the best opportunity to examine the relevance of an applicant's knowledge, skill and experience fit for the job.

LinkedIn Groups: Through this LinkedIn groups, group of professionals can share various information among themselves.

Literature Survey: It is the essential segment of any credible research. Survey of existing literature is essential to be informed about the latest research in the area of investigation, which helps to give a theoretical foundation to the article.

Mass Communication: This is mainly the application of tools of mass media.

Media Communication: The main tools for media communication are computers, cell phones, LCD, video, television etc. Presently internet has become very accepted for this communication.

Memorandum: A memorandum (memo) is the most commonly use of communication within an organization. In establishments and offices, memos are used to circulate the information to the employees regarding the happenings in the company.

Methodology: While writing a technical article, it is necessary to mention the methods and materials to be used to conduct the investigation. In order to establish the validity of the findings, the materials and methods used need to be described along with the justification for using them. This may involve the research design, research procedures, kind of data, data collection procedure, and the criteria of survey.

MMS: It stands for "Multimedia Messaging Service" It is an accepted messaging service in the field of communication. Also considered as a latest and prominent wireless standard for multimedia.

Movie Film Projector: This medium is now being used not only for entertainment but also for teaching, training and advertising

Nomenclature: It is a devising of names for things. The nomenclature list should be in alphabetical order (capital letter first and then lower case letters) followed by any Greek symbols identified with headings.

Non Statutory Report: Non-statutory reports are made not because of legal compulsion but because of necessity.

Non-verbal Barriers: Various factors can result in being the barriers to non-verbal communication affecting the business processes and efficiency of the organization.

Nonverbal Communication: In this communication, a message is been communicated without using a word.

Notes: Preparing notes is a vital study skill that is essential for various academics and professional purpose. It is a methodical way of writing a text quickly, briefly, and clearly.

Oral Communication: In oral communication the sender and the receiver interact face to face.

Overhead Projector: It is a popular audio visual tool which is versatile in nature and relatively inexpensive aid to the speaker.

Paralanguage: It is the way inflections are used when sending a message verbally. It reflects in the overall attitude of a person, his pitch, tone of voice, and the volume while communicating.

Pinterest: It is one type of social network that permits users to share and find out new interests by posting images or videos to their own or others' boards and browsing what other users have pinned.

Power Point Presentation: It is one of the most widely used packages is Power Point. Power point presentation enables to create a document called presentation which is used for communicating ideas, thoughts and messages to the audience.

Proof Reading: It means revising the earlier one to make it better. In proof reading the corrections in grammar, spelling and punctuation has to be done carefully.

Psychological Pattern: The speeches structured in the Psychological Pattern are quite emotive in style and sense.

Psychometric test: To judge a candidate personality, very often, psychometric tests are administered.

Public Speaking: Public speaking means speaking to a group of persons or audience on a subject that is professional in nature.

Reduction Devices: This is unique technique to reduce the expression. Reduction devices are mainly use in 'Abbreviations' and 'Symbols'.

Reference: It is the complete information about the sources from where the author has referred to his/her writing.

RFID: "Radio Frequency Identification" are chips that respond to "radio waves" with encoded information, allowing companies to tag and track items and materials.

Routine Report: Routine report is made and presented to the director at particular intervals.

Schematizing: It is the technique of using graphics to organize notes.

Semantic or Language Gap: Sometimes the gap arises because much of what people say is subjective or multiple meaning of words or misinterpretation of language.

Skill Assessment: Skill assessment is the unique process of analysing the skills of a candidate appearing for a job interview.

SMS: Full form **is "Short Message Services"** and broadly used features on mobile phone and is considered as a trusted communication tool.

Solicited Proposals: These are written in response to a specific request from a client. In many cases, a standard format is provided to the parties to submit their proposals.

Specific Report: This report is made and presented to the top level management on specific request.

Statutory Report: Statutory reports are prepared in order to fulfil the legal compliance.

Stress Interview: The candidate is asked a series of questions rapidly to assess his/her capability to handle the stressed situations

Research Article: It is based on original research carried out by the authors.

Review Article: A review article is an evaluation and analysis of published work on a particular topic.

Technical Article: It is basically a written composition which describes, discuss, or analyze a systematic investigation towards increasing the sum of knowledge on a specific field.

Technical Proposals: It is written by someone who needs to sort out a technical, management or business problem or needs to implement new ideas to enhance productivity in various professional operations. Proposals have important role in business growth and professional relationships.

Telephonic Interview: This is a common form of interview process. This is specially conducted when the candidate does not reside near the prospective employer.

Technical Interview: This is an essential round of screening. In this process of interview, the experts of the panel try to find out the technical knowledge of the interviewee.

Teleconferencing: This is live "real time session" among multiple participants and can listen and see to each other with the facility of sharing data.

Title: It is the first component of all technical articles.

Topical Pattern: It is a commonly used pattern is the Topical Pattern where different parts of speech have to divide and arrange and plot them into various heading and sub headings.

Transcribing: It is writing down verbatim what is said.

Tropicalizing: It refers to write a word or phrase to represent a section of the text.

Twitter: It is also one kind of social network through which an individual or a group of individuals may express their opinions or status with a short message. The character limit of short message is 140.

Unsolicited Proposals: They are more detailed and should draw the attention of the receiver. These proposals are based on an objective assessment of a situation or condition by an individual or a firm.

Upward Communication: It includes the transmission of information from the subordinates to their seniors.

Variation in Language: Sometimes the words and expression are culture specific. If it is not been used properly it might lead barriers in communication process.

VCD and DVD Players: Any display material requiring visual motion and sound can be recorded or downloaded on a compact disc (CD) and used for presentation on VCD or DVD players.

Verbal Barriers: Verbal barriers are verbal attach, speaking loudly and using complex words.

Verbal Communication: A professional person has to deal his /her prime working time in speaking and listening to other person apart from reading and writing.

Video Conferencing: It is a visual conference between two or more individuals in spite of their location, featuring audio and video content communication in real time.

WeChat: It is a messaging app where you can only consider region and ethnicity.

Bibliography

Books:

Agnihotri, R.K. and Khanna, A.L. (1997). *Problematizing English in India*. New Delhi, Sage Publications.

Angel, Pamela. (2004) *Business Design.* Irwin/McGraw-Hill, New York.

Arnold and George T. (2010) *Media Writer's Handbook: A guide to Common Writing and Editing Problems.* Tata McGraw Hill Publishing Company Limited, New Delhi.

Austin, J.L., (1962). *How to Do Things with Words*. Harward University Press, Cambridge

Basu, B.N. (2007) *Technical Writing.* Prentice-Hall of India, New Delhi.

Bhatanager, R.P. and R.T. Bell, (2004). *Communication in English.* Orient Longman, Hyderabad.

Chaturvedi, P.D and M.Chaturvedi. (2008) *Business Communication Concepts, Cases and Applications.* Pearson Education, Delhi.

Curtis, D.B., J.L.Winsor, and R.D.Stephens. (1989) *National Preferences in Business and Communication Education.* Tata McGraw-Hill, New York Finder.

Eastwood, John (2005) *Grammar Finder.* Oxford University Press, Oxford.

Freeman, S. (1997). *Written Communication in English*, Orient Longman, Hyderabad.

Guffey, Mary Ellen. (2004) *Essentials of Business Communication.* Melissa Acuna, USA.

Halliday, M. A.K., (1973). *Explorations in the Functions of Language.* Edward Arnold, London.

Inthira, S.R. and V.Saraswathi, (1995). *Enrich Your English Communication Skills Book*, OUP, New Delhi.

Jadeja, R. and S. Natraj, (2004). *Communicative Approach*. Gurjar Sahitya Bhavan, Ahmedabad

Jones, Leo and Richard Alexander, (1996) *New International Business English: Communication skills in English for Business Purposes.* Cambridge University Press, Cambridge.

Kaul, Asha. (2010) *Business Communication*. PHI Learning, New Delhi.

Koneru, Aruna. (2006) *Business Communication and Report Writing.* ICFAI University Press. Hyderabad

Krizan, A.C.et al. (2008) *Effective Business Communication.* Cengage Learning. New Delhi.

Kumar, S and Lata Pushp. (2011) *Communication Skills.* Oxford University Press, New Delhi.

Lata, Pushp and Sanjay Kumar. (2010) *Communicate to Conquer: A Hand book of Group Discussions and Interviews.* Printice –Hall of India Learning. New Delhi.

Lata, Pushp and Sanjay Kumar. (2007) *Communicate or Collapse: A Hand book of Effective Public Speaking, Group Discussion and Interviews.* Printice –Hall of India Learning. New Delhi.

Lehman, C.M. and D.D.Dufrene. (1999) *Business Communication.* Cincinnati.

Lesikar, and Pettett. (2001) *Essentials of Business Communication.* Tata McGraw Hill Publishing Company Limited, New Delhi.

Lesikar, Raymond V.et al. (2009) *Business Communication.* Tata McGraw Hill Publishing Company Limited, New York

Lewis, Norman. (1994) *Word Power Made Easy.* Goyel Saab Publishers and Distributers, Delhi

Locker, Kitty O and Stephen Kyo Kaczmarek. (2007) *Business Communication.* Tata McGraw Hill Publishing Company Limited, New Delhi.

Mitra, Barun K. (2006) *Effective Technical Communication: A Guide for Scientists and Engineers.* Oxford University Press, New Delhi.

Mitra, C.R. (1989). *Education for Self-reliance: Alternatives in Education and Development.* Association of Indian Universities, New Delhi

Mohan, Krishna and Meera Banerji. (1990) *Developing Communication Skills.* Macmillan India Limited, New Delhi

Monipally, Matthukutty M. (2001) *Business Communication Strategies.* Tata McGraw Hill Publishing Company Limited, New Delhi.

Murphy, A. Herta, and Peck, E. Charrles. (2008) *Effective Business Communication.* Tata McGraw Hill Publishing Company Limited, New Delhi.

Pal, Rajindra and Korlahalli, J. S. (2012) Essentials *of Business Communication.* Sultan Chand and Sons, New Delhi.

Pattensheti, C. C. (2003) Business *Communication.* R. Chand and Company Publishers, New Delhi.

Prasad. (1998) *Communication Skills for Engineers and Professionals.* S.K. Kataria & Sons, Delhi

Ramen, Meenakshi and S. Sharma. (2004) *Technical Communication: Principles and Practice.* Oxford University Press, New Delhi.

Rao, E. Nageswara. (1992) *New Horizons in Teaching English.* Academic Foundation. Delhi

Riordan, Daniel G.and Steven E.Pauley (2004) *Technical Report Writing Today*. Biztantra .New Delhi

Rizvi, M.Ashraf. (2005) *Effective Technical Communication.* Tata McGraw Hill Publishing Company Limited, New Delhi.

Sasikumar, V. and V. Syamala, (2003). *Form and Function: A Communicative Grammar for Colleges.* Emerald Publishers, Chennai.

Sethi, J.A. (2007) *A Handbook of Standard English and Indian Usage.* Prentice-Hall of India, New Delhi.

Sharma, R.C. and Krishna Mohan.(2010) *Business Correspondence and Report Writing.* Tata McGraw Hill Publishing Company Limited, New Delhi.

Sharma, Sangeeta and Binod Mishra. (2009) *Communication Skills for Engineers and Scientists* PHI Learning, New Delhi.

Sinha, K. K. (2012) *Business Communication.* Galgotia Publishing Company, New Delhi.

Soti, S.C. and R.K. Sharma, (2002). *Research in Education.* Atlantic, New Delhi.

Stephen, E. Lucas. (2001) *The Art of Public Speaking*. Tata McGraw Hill Publishing Company Limited, Singapore.

Unpublished Dissertations and Theses:

Deshmukh, V., (1997). Development of a Need Based Course in English Language for some Polytechnic Departments of S.N.D.T. Women's University, Unpublished Ph.D. Thesis, SNDT Mumbai.

Kale, A., (2001). A Study of the Writing Skills Component at the Second Year Functional English Course in the University of Pune, M.Phil., Unpublished Dissertation, CIEFL

Pramanik, T. K., (1988). A Study of Some Affective Variables related to Learning English as a Second Language at the Post-Secondary Stage in Orissa, Unpublished Ph.D. Thesis, CIEFL.

Research Articles & Journals:

Arnold, V. & Roach, T. (1992). Organizational behavior: Coping with difficult co-workers. Journal of Education for Business, 67(3), 160-163.

Burger, C. (1995). Why should they believe us? Communication World, 12(1), 16-17.

Caudron, S. (1996). Angry employees bite back in court. Personnel Journal, 75(12), December, 32-37.

Gerber, G. (1996). Problem personalities: Employees who drive us up a wall. Getting Results, 41(12), December, 5.

Grimsley, K. (1999). When life at work gets hairy: U.S. agency calls on-the-job stress a rising threat to employee health. The Washington Post, January 6,

Johnson, D., Kurutz, J. & Kiehlbauch, J. (1995). Scenario for supervisors. Magazine, 40(2), February, 63-67.

Marsh, C. & Arnold, V. (1988). Address the cause, not the symptoms of behavior problems. Personnel Journal, 67(5), May, 92-98.